ALL 1 HAVE SEEN...

A record of the past;
A prophecy for the future.

"If it be marvelous in the eyes of the remnant of this
people in these days, should it also be marvelous in mine
eyes, says the Lord of Hosts?"

The Prophet Zechariah
Chap. 8, v.6

The Right Reverend Arthur R. McKinstry, D.D.
Fifth Bishop of Delaware
1939–1954

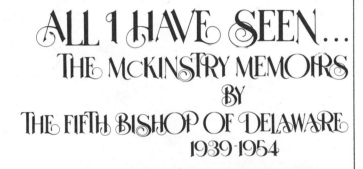

ALL 1 HAVE SEEN...
THE MCKINSTRY MEMOIRS
BY
THE FIFTH BISHOP OF DELAWARE
1939-1954

Serendipity Press
Wilmington, Delaware 19807

PRINTED IN THE UNITED STATES OF AMERICA
Designed By Edward J. Bonner

ACKNOWLEDGMENTS

The Author would like to express gratitude to William P. Frank, Columnist of the News-Journal newspapers, for his encouragement and editorial advice. His thanks to Mrs. Nathalie K. Battis, Secretary of the Convention, Diocese of Delaware, for her diligence in manuscript preparation; also a word of appreciation to Ellice McDonald for guidance and assistance.

We are grateful to Sports Illustrated for permission to excerpt from "Faith and Form at Saratoga" by Whitney Tower which appeared in the August 16, 1965 issue.

Photograph of Colonel Elliot courtesy of Wm. Shewell Ellis Studios. Photograph of Mr. Haskell and Bishop McKinstry courtesy of Willard Stewart, Inc. Photograph of St. Andrews School courtesy of Brooks Studio. Photograph of Bishop McKinstry and Mrs. Richard C. duPont courtesy of New York Racing Assn. Inc., Photographer: Paul Schafer.

Dedication

TO MOLLY LAIRD DOWNS

It has been said that God and one dedicated child of His are "a majority" when it comes to dealing with the challenging issues of life. If that be true, then God and three or four persons in love with His Kingdom might possibly be a "landslide".

During the crucial years of my ministry in Delaware, when the momentum of the Diocesan program was picking up, Molly Downs and her husband, Ellason, opened their home on Lancaster Pike, just outside of Wilmington, to the monthly meetings of the Diocesan Executive Council. Molly served what she called "Bishop's Brew" (enlivened tea) and she spiced the meetings with her well-known wit. Her brother-in-law, Robert N. Downs, III, encouraged, of course, by his wonderful wife, Letty, made up the Downs' team on the Council.

Molly Downs' good works have long been known. For many years she has given extensive financial support to the Virginia Theological Seminary in Alexandria, Virginia. She has also sent generous offerings to widely diversified missionary projects throughout the world. Her generosity to the Diocese of Delaware has been most helpful.

We salute Molly—a brave, plucky, loyal soldier of Christ—and we humbly dedicate this book to this outstanding churchwoman, and to her faith, her courage and her patience. It was she who once humorously suggested that the memoirs of the fifth Bishop of Delaware be entitled "Mac's Tracks"—because they dealt with a ministry that covered an unusual number of people and exciting events, from New England to Texas and most places between.

God bless Molly Laird Downs. May her eloquent witness inspire ever greater numbers of people.

Arthur R. McKinstry
Fifth Bishop of Delaware
1975

Contents

The Publisher Notes

Only occasionally does one meet a man whose career has been replete with successive triumphs—each combining devotion to God with an extraordinary understanding of humanity. Such a man is Arthur R. McKinstry, fifth Bishop of Delaware.

The title of his book of Memoirs comes from a quotation by Ralph Waldo Emerson: *"All I Have Seen* teaches me to trust the Creator for all I have not seen". It is ideally suited, for Bishop McKinstry has "Seen" and perceived, if you will, so much along the byways and intersections of his eighty-one years.

Reading of his experiences makes one wonder how a man of the cloth could also become involved in shaping so many diversified peoples' lives—whether churchman or agnostic, white or black, Episcopal, Catholic or Judiac. How was he able to cover so much ground? Perhaps the quintessence of his success can be understood by knowing that early in life he seems to have found the key to most human motivations—the many frailties of individuals and, above all, the knowledge that there is an underlying goodness in most everyone. He had the adroitness to inspire trust, and was therefore able to fight ignorance.

The McKinstry Memoirs are candid and revealing. Brimming with facts, anecdotes and colorful personalities—this autobiography captures the full flavor of a high-powered gentleman. His book never stands still. There are fascinating vignettes of his family life. The story told is weighty in intent, graceful in tone, witty and historically significant.

The Bishop remains an optimist, and doesn't believe the world is coming to an end. He writes: "In the next fifty years America will return to religion. This country will become, in the eyes of the world, a spiritually-minded nation again . . . the threats to world peace will pass. The United Nations Organization, with a greater understanding among peoples, will finally act effectively . . . nations will come to understand the importance of interdependence and cooperation . . ."

The Foreword to the McKinstry Memoirs was written by the distinguished churchman, Joseph W. Chinn, Jr., who served for twenty-two years (under three Bishops) as one of the seven man Board of Trustees for the Episcopal Diocese.

The career of Bishop McKinstry, and the man himself, will indeed be a legend in Delaware for a long, long time.

Serendipity Press is proud of the opportunity to publish *All I Have Seen*.

J. Blan van Urk

Foreword

These memoirs are facets in a brilliant and constructive career in the ministry of the Protestant Episcopal Church.

The author's qualities of leadership, personality, compassion, dedication, energy and humor would have guaranteed him success in any other field—whether professional, political or business. It was fortuitous that he chose the ministry, for the State of Delaware was greatly enriched by his installation as the fifth Bishop of the Episcopal Diocese. During his episcopacy, from 1939 to 1954, I would hesitate to guess the thousands of miles he traveled up and down this small state, putting his touch where it was needed.

In retirement, "Bishop Mac", as he is respectfully and affectionately known, continues to inspire his "flock" as a great Christian leader and a friend to all. Truly, it can be said he has sparked the modern day renaissance among clergy and laymen which today forms the basic strength of our National church.

Joseph W. Chinn, Jr.

Wilmington, Delaware
1975

Chapter 1

An Unheralded Arrival

It was on Sunday, February 12, 1939, at eleven p.m. that I arrived in Wilmington, Delaware at the well regarded Hotel Du Pont. I was accompanied by my wife Isabelle, and our five children, Isabelle, Margaret, Barbara, James and Arthur—all of us completely worn-out after a tedious motor trip from our home in Nashville, Tennessee, by way of Florida.

Friday, February 17, had been set as the day of consecration of the fifth Bishop of Delaware, in the Cathedral Church of St. John, Wilmington. Only five days remained for settling into old Bishopstead on West Fourteenth Street, where all the Delaware Bishops had lived since the establishment of the Diocese.

As the weary group approached the hotel desk, I—the Bishop to be—neglected to identify myself, and as I was in mufti, the desk clerk had no idea who I was.

"How much for three rooms—father, mother, three girls and two boys?"

It never occurred to me that Colonel George A. Elliott and his welcoming committee might have alerted the management to look out for us and to receive us as guests of the diocese. So, I did not identify myself. I seldom do. The desk clerk was very polite. He named a price which, to a man who had just spent too much in Florida at the tag-end of the Great Depression, was staggering. Gathering my clan, I went out the door, mumbling that I did not intend to buy the hotel.

I asked the doorman, a big fellow resplendent in uniform, to direct me to another hotel in Wilmington. He looked at me rather strangely. He undoubtedly expected me to know that the Hotel du Pont was the only fine hotel in Delaware and famous in this country and abroad—owned and operated by the Du Pont Company.

Regaining his composure the doorman coolly informed me that the Hotel Darling was a block away on Market Street, right around the corner, and he haughtily dismissed me to my fate.

This hotel received us quite cordially. It was nothing like the Hotel du Pont, but, it was clean looking, and it provided three lovely rooms on the top floor for a total price of $11 per night. Quite a saving! Exhausted as we were, the family promptly tumbled into bed for a wonderful rest.

The next morning, we trooped down Market Street to the corner of Tenth Street and perched on stools in the old United Cigar Store, the location now of the handsome Farmers' Bank. There we had our first breakfast in Wilmington and we were content.

Later in the morning, I telephoned Colonel Elliott and he was horrified to learn that the Bishop-Elect and his family had begun their Delaware adventure in a hotel whose status was somewhat below the one they had planned for us. Picking us up soon after, Colonel Elliott took us to his pet institution, the YMCA at the corner of Washington and Eleventh Streets. We had our first Wilmington lunch at the "Y", where we met Alva E. Lindley, who was the General Secretary at that time and who, incidentally, along with his wife, Alice, remained a very dear friend of mine all through the years.

In a day or so we were safely lodged in the ancient Bishopstead on the Brandywine. The house had been built in 1741 by the Canby family, and it had been owned after their occupancy by Bishop Alfred Lee, the first Bishop of Delaware, who had named it "Ingleside". He lived in this expansive house until his death in 1888.

Following the death of the first Bishop, the

The Old Bishopstead—From a painting by Frank Schoonover

house was purchased by Francis G. du Pont. He turned it over to the Diocese of Delaware to be used as the residence of all subsequent Bishops.

The first Bishop to occupy the "Bishopstead", following the death of Bishop Lee, was the Right Reverend Leighton Coleman, who had married the sister of Francis G. du Pont. He was succeeded there by the third Bishop of Delaware, the Right Reverend Frederick J. Kinsman and his mother and sister, and later, the Right Reverend Philip Cook, and his family.

It was Bishop Coleman who built the beautiful chapel at the end of the library, a design he had copied from a chapel in England. It was greatly used throughout the ministries of Bishop Coleman and his successors. Bishop Coleman and Bishop Kinsman entertained generously at Bishopstead. The latter made it his policy to invite all of the people who had been confirmed during the previous year to a garden party in the spring. Bishop Coleman and his wife inaugurated annual affairs on the grounds of Bishopstead for the benefit of St. Michael's Day Nursery on Washington Street.

By the time Bishop Cook came to Delaware this home was renowned and beloved throughout the state, since many Delawareans, some of them quite prominent, had been baptized, confirmed and married in the lovely chapel. When they died, Bishop Coleman and Bishop Cook lay in state in the chapel just prior to the funeral services. During my time, when I alighted from a train and hailed a taxi, I needed only to say to the driver, "Bishopstead, please." The house had become that well known.

So, ensconced high on the banks of the rushing waters of historic Brandywine Creek, the family of the Bishop-Elect, not long departed from the arid lands of Texas, were settled, and extremely happy.

Our welcome to Delaware had been warm and enthusiastic. The front page of the *Journal Every Evening* on February 17, the day of the consecration, carried photographs of the procession over four columns, with a two-column spread of news describing the service. This was continued on a subsequent page and covered a full eight-column page with pictures and news stories about the new Bishop, the three consecrators, and the Cathedral Church of St. John itself. This simply has to be the greatest publicity any Bishop-Elect ever received. And it does seem in strange contrast with the paucity of publicity devoted to churches these days.

In preparation for the consecration service, my wife's beloved Aunt Adelaide, accompanied by Mrs. Margaret A. Baer, and my wife's sister, Mrs. Martha Andrews, arrived from Cleveland, the home of my wife's family since Cleveland's earliest. They immediately loved Bishopstead but were frightened by a local phenomenon: the steady stream of "bums" who found their way to Bishopstead each night to beg cash to help them "get to Chester".

Indeed, I learned that these poor souls had been waiting in line for weeks for the coming of the new Bishop. It is to Bishop Cook's everlasting credit that he never turned anyone away from Bishopstead who came requesting money. He always provided the cash to help "the men get to Chester".

I had a different way of handling such cases. I had been very well trained by social workers in several large city parishes. And so I established credit at the Sunday Morning Breakfast Mission and at the Salvation Army. Whenever anyone came to me for help, I would say, "I do not have any cash in this house—and I will never have any—but if you're in need of lodging and food, here are some cards. I've made arrangements with these institutions to take care of you and they will be glad to do it—and will do it well."

It seems that they didn't want anything but money. Whether they wanted it for transportation to

Chester, or for liquor, or for something else, I never quite knew. But in a remarkably short time these strange, somewhat frightening night callers entirely disappeared.

We all liked Delaware on sight. The country surrounding Wilmington must be described as the most beautifully cultivated in the nation—a statement that will probably create great debate on the part of those who love other areas better. I do know that very soon it became my daily routine, after depositing my children in school, to spend an hour exploring the roads around my new See City.

Wilmington had a population in 1939 of 106,000. New Castle County had approximately 130,000 and the population of the entire state was 238,000. People in those years had no idea of the miraculous population growth which Wilmington and New Castle County, and other areas, would experience in the decades ahead. I recently asked a prominent real estate agent if he had ever anticipated the prosperity he had enjoyed in recent years. Laughingly he said, "Indeed not."

I found the entire state, and its three counties— New Castle, Kent and Sussex, most charming. I reveled in the capital city of Dover, then a town of 5,000 population, and in later years my wife and I always attended Dover Day.

Newark, which by now has become quite a city, in 1939 was a modest little place, the site of a small university. Sussex County could boast of its lovely beaches and coastal areas. Rehoboth had but a handful of year-round residents. In the summertime, of course, many people moved down from upper Delaware into their own homes or rented homes for the season. Gradually thousands started coming to Rehoboth from Washington and western Pennsylvania.

I had, I found, inherited a "tight" little diocese, possessing many charming features and a population proud of its history and totally unaware of the dramatic growth to come.

And so now, the McKinstrys were a part of all this loveliness, this history, this place where the nation had begun. We were now ready for the big event—the consecration. But all this we had nearly passed up.

Chapter 2

Consecration:
Fifth Bishop of Delaware

Friday, February 17, 1939, dawned clear but cold. Everything was in readiness at the Cathedral Church of St. John. Paul Terry, the official organist and choirmaster, ruled supreme over every detail. The service was scheduled for ten thirty in the morning. Every seat was filled. It was the most moving service of my life.

The Presiding Bishop, the Right Reverend Henry St. George Tucker, was the Consecrator, assisted by the Bishop of Bethlehem, the Right Reverend Frank W. Sterrett, and also the Bishop of Tennessee, the Right Reverend James M. Maxon. The Right Reverend G. Ashton Oldham, the Bishop of Albany—a Bishop of mine during the years 1927 through 1931—was the preacher, the Right Reverend R. Bland Mitchell of Arkansas and the Right Reverend Frederick D. Goodwin of Virginia were the Bishops selected to present me.

The Reverend Doctor Roelif H. Brooks, rector of St. Thomas' Church, Fifth Avenue, New York, and my predecessor in Albany, and the Reverend Richard W. Trapnell, former rector of St. Andrew's Church, Wilmington—then resident in Long Island—were my attending presbyters.

Also participating were Bishop Ernest M. Stires of Long Island, Bishop W. B. Stevens of Los Angeles, Bishop E. B. Dendridge, my immediate predecessor in Nashville and now Bishop Coadjutor of that diocese,

L. to R., Bishop Arthur R. McKinstry, Reverend Richard W. Trapnell,
Bishop Henry St. George Tucker

The Cathedral Church of St. John

Bishop W. Appleton Lawrence of Western Massachusetts, and Bishop S. Harrington Littell of Honolulu whose father had once been the rector of St. John's Cathedral where I was being consecrated. Also present was Bishop J. C. Ward of Erie, Pennsylvania. Bishop Manning, who at the last moment found he was unable to attend, sent his affectionate greetings.

Following the Service of Consecration a great crowd of people pressed around me. One man who approached me was the dean of a prominent cathedral in the east. He knelt to kiss my ring and request my apostolic blessing. Since I am a person with a Presbyterian and Quaker background and not given to much ostentation, I lifted him quickly from his knees and bade him accompany me upstairs to my private vesting room. I was not about to give a blessing with a great crowd pressing all around me. This little incident shows how times have changed. Ostentation is more the rule than the exception today.

After the service at the cathedral, there was a luncheon in the Gold Ballroom of the Hotel Du Pont, with the president of the University of Delaware, Doctor Walter Hullihen, serving as toastmaster. Because all my children attended the luncheon (including little Arthur, who was rather wigglesome at the time) my wife had insisted on occupying a table at the back of the ballroom, where she could sit with the children, keep an eye on young Arthur, and be with her Aunt Adelaide and her sister, Martha Andrews.

This was probably the only time in all my experience that the wife of a newly consecrated Bishop did not sit at the head table. I introduced her and the others when I myself was recognized.

The preceding speeches had been pleasant and witty, becoming such an occasion, and in speaking to my new flock, I stressed my desire to get to know them and to visit their homes. I warned them, in a rather light vein and somewhat casually, that they would find me very informal, apt to show up unannounced. Moreover, I cautioned, if I could raise no one at the front entrance to the house, I would arrive at the kitchen door.

Later I heard that my remarks had upset some of the southern Delaware people, who—having heard Bill Frank's broadcast from the organ loft during the consecration service—thought I had failed to give them proper credit for being as formal and as well-living as the residents of New Castle County. Of course, such a thought was never in my mind. But the incident did put me on guard as to the sensitiveness of some of my flock in certain portions of the state at that time.

Thus I had been launched in my challenging and demanding new calling as Bishop of Delaware. I knew I faced a difficult job. There had been no diocesan Bishop since late 1937, and the backlog of pastoral responsibilities was large and rather staggering.

What kind of a diocese had I inherited? It would take a considerable time to discover an adequate answer to this question. I knew that Delaware's brand of churchmanship would be quite congenial to me. I had been consecrated on Friday, and a few churchmen present at the luncheon following the consecration had professed shock when the luncheon committee had served them roast lamb. Although the toastmaster, Doctor Hullihen, seemed to be quite horrified by this error, I think he was a bit surprised that anybody in the diocese would complain. But he was overly anxious about this, since there were very few strict churchmen in the Diocese of Delaware in 1939.

[11]

Delaware always had a number of old-fashioned high churchmen—but probably very few Anglo-Catholics. Because of my rearing I knew a great deal about high church life and practice. My personal preference and background inhibited me, however, from any form of extremism. As to other characteristics of my new diocese, it would take time before I would know the facts.

My first sermon was preached on Sunday, February 19, at Immanuel Church in Wilmington at the special request of the rector, the Reverend Doctor Charles W. Clash, president of the standing committee of the diocese. Since he had been twice defeated for the bishopric of Delaware I naturally wondered what kind of a reception I would receive in his parish. But he was truly gracious. The church was crowded. My sermon topic was "What is Christianity?". The people were very warm in their response.

On Monday, February 20, the Church Club of Delaware gave the McKinstrys a reception at the Hotel Du Pont. About 500 attended. We were able to meet many people from all over the state and I counted this event a very important part of my learning process.

On Thursday, February 23, the Reverend Doctor Joseph H. Earp, then the rector of Immanuel Church, New Castle, the mother church of the diocese, founded in 1704, came for me in his car. We went to call on many of his parishioners in New Castle and also on the then superintendent of the New Castle schools, Dr. Samuel Burr. I loved this experience because during my rectorships I had greatly enjoyed visiting people in their homes and offices.

Thus I began a quiet study of my new diocese. As I pondered the situation, it seemed to me quite likely that in a small diocese like Delaware, the Bishop could know as many of his people as he desired. I resolved I would get to know as many as the limitations of time and responsibility would allow. And ultimately I would get into their homes. I simply couldn't stop being a parish rector, a pastoral minister, even though the church had elevated me to an administrative position. I fully realized, however, that I must never come between a rector and his people or weaken the rector's relationships in any way. I was very strict about observing the independence and sovereignity of the rector, since I was convinced then— and still am—that the strength of a diocese depends, in a large measure, upon the closeness of the parish clergy to their own people. This would ever be my guiding principle as Bishop.

I had begun my service in the Diamond State. It was a beautiful place, and we were at home there—but I had almost passed it up.

How was that? Well, that is part of my story and recollections. If my friends will bear with me, we will start from the beginning of a life that has been rich in experiences—devotion and love of family and friends, and a richness that was more than I deserved.

[13]

Chapter 3

The Beginning

During my ministry as a parish priest, I had never had a small parish or lived in a small town. My parishes were all city parishes, some of them very large. It would be fair to say that a Bishop who had served exclusively in large city parishes might find it difficult to minister to small town congregations or to rural areas and be happy among such people. This possibility never occurred to me during my active episcopate; however, in the years since, it has more than once come to my mind. The Diocese of Delaware was, in fact, taking a risk by electing a city parish parson to Delaware, where many of the parishes were in small towns.

I think the answer is that my life and training as a boy was in a small Kansas parish. There I learned to worship. I also learned that people are greatly beloved of God and regardless of the size of the town or the parish, the parson is ordained and called to be the Shepherd of the Flock. In a small parish he can do this, if he dares and if he cares, much better than he can in a city parish.

But what had been my background? Where had I come from?

I was born on July 26, 1894 in the small Kansas town of Greeley—no doubt named for Horace Greeley—whose most famous cliche was "Go west, young man. Go west." My family had heeded Greeley's admonition.

My grandfather, William Orlando McKinstry, was born in Hyde Park, Vermont, in the year 1834. This branch of the family had moved from Massachusetts to

Bishop Arthur R. McKinstry's Birthplace, Greeley, Kansas

Vermont shortly after the Revolutionary War. (I might note that I had a relative in most of the skirmishes and battles of the Revolution.)

Some of the McKinstry men, with their compatriots in the war and with the members of their families, had gone—not west yet—but north to Vermont. There, they founded the town of Hyde Park. In later years I went to visit this town with my two sons, Jim and Arthur, and we identified the site of my ancestors' home on what is known today as "McKinstry Hill".

After some years there, my grandfather, having reached maturity, tired of the confining economic restrictions of the area, and decided to "go west". First, he married Miss Evelyn Brownell of Quaker background. They lived in Illinois for several years but ultimately they headed for Hall's Summit, Kansas, where my grandfather bought a large farm. He worked the place with diligence and skill for many years, and died there.

I used to visit that hospitable farm in my boyhood days. I remember so well how Grandmother McKinstry, a wonderful cook, served breakfasts of hot oatmeal, eggs, bacon, buckwheat cakes and delicious home-made sausage delicately flavored with sage.

The Kansas McKinstrys were far from their New England ancestral home. My first ancestor to arrive in New England was Captain George Barbour, who came from Land's End, England, in 1635. We have evidence that he was a very helpful citizen in the Massachusetts Bay Colony. He helped organize the military department of the colonial government and served for many terms as a deputy to their government.

The first McKinstry—William—came to this country in 1742. He married Moriah Morse, granddaughter of Captain Barbour. His bride was also a decendant of one Henry Adams. The New England McKinstrys intermarried with the Adams family, the Morse, Noyes and Wood families of Massachusetts.

William Orlando McKinstry's mother was Miriam St. Clair. She was the daughter of James St. Clair. The St. Clairs had emigrated from Scotland.

The first St. Clair—William—had come from Normandy with his uncle, William the Conqueror. His father, the Earl of Clare, had cautioned his son that he might not get along too well with Uncle Willie. Young William decided before long (sometime after 1066) to take the letters from his father to King Malcolm and Queen Margaret of Scotland. They liked the young man so well that he was made the Queen's Royal Cup Bearer, and later, the first Prince and Earl of the Orkney Islands. He was also given lands south of Edinburgh centering at Rosslyn.

The third Prince and Earl of Orkney—also Sir William, who was the first grand master of the Masonic Lodge in Scotland—built the castle and the beautiful chapel. The castle has long since been largely destroyed (probably by Cromwell), but the chapel built in 1450 still stands. It has the most beautiful stone carvings in Britain, and although it seats fewer than a hundred people it took fifty years to build. Queen Victoria ordered that the chapel must forever be kept in perfect repair. The buildings and land are still owned by the St. Clairs—now known as St. Clair-Erskine, the Earl of Rosslyn. Rosslyn Chapel has been written about in English literature by such notables as Milton, Wordsworth and Sir Walter Scott, in his "Lay of the Last Minstrel".

Some of the St. Clairs left Scotland for the New World. Arthur St. Clair, for whom I and my son, Arthur, were named, went to Canada to serve as an officer in the British army, fighting on the plains of Abraham.

When he resigned his commission, he went for a while to Boston where he became a very popular figure and married Phoebe Bayard, the niece of the Governor of the Massachusetts Bay Colony. The couple went to western Pennsylvania to establish their home and also to build the area's first grist mills. When the Revolution flared, George Washington appealed to Arthur to join the army and use his skills for the colonies. He did so, and became a prominent general.

He had a cousin, James, and these men had offspring, ergo the St. Clairs in the new country. My great grandfather of New England was also named James St. Clair—a name not unknown in national newspapers as recently as 1974.

To return to the McKinstrys in Kansas: Grandfather Orlando and his wife, Evelyn Brownell, left three heirs—Arthur, Leslie, born in 1870, and Howard. Neither Uncle Arthur nor my father, Leslie, cared for farming. In fact my father had grieved his parents greatly by going off to college to study architecture and music.

My mother, Cevilla Surbeck, who had also moved to Hall's Summit, Kansas with her family, was born in Ohio in 1872, near Toledo. She was the daughter of a Swiss gentleman, George Surbeck, whose family had come to the United States from Shaffhausen, a town near Zurich, a little before the War between the States. He was my favorite grandparent. He was charming, witty and quite brilliant. He was always interested in children. He used to sit with me by the hour as if I were an adult, and discuss important events in world affairs, politics at home and abroad. In Switzerland his family had been very active in matters of church and state. In America the Surbeck's had first lived near Clyde, Ohio, where George had married Elizabeth Wicks, whose origins were Dutch, and together they had moved to Kansas, to live near Hall's Summit.

Leslie Irving, the second son of William Orlando, married beautiful Cevilla Surbeck on March 17, 1890. They lived in Burlington, Kansas, twelve miles from Hall's Summit, the home of their respective parents.

My older brother Clarence Elroy was born in Burlington in 1891, my only sister, Mildred, in Paola,

Kansas, May 8, 1897. While I was yet a small boy, the family moved to Kansas City where my father, a competent pianist and organist, became the choirmaster and organist at St. Mary's Episcopal Church in that city. This was considered a "high church" even in those days. I can well remember the lighting and extinguishing of many, many candles and the obnoxious fragrance of incense.

I was only about two years old when my parents began taking me to religious services in Kansas City. The effect of these services remained with me all through my boyhood years and long afterwards. I have always believed parents should take their young children to church with them, because youngsters absorb far more than adults realize. The services at Old St. Mary's quickened my sense of awe, an essential ingredient in religion. The idea of the holy is absolutely required.

One day my father came to the conclusion that rearing a family in a big city was far from ideal. He therefore moved to Independence, Missouri, where he became organist and choirmaster at Trinity Church. Dad taught Bess Wallace (later to become Mrs. Harry Truman) in Sunday School and trained her in a junior choir. He became well acquainted with the Wallaces and the Trumans.

After some years there, we moved to Coffeyville, Kansas, situated on the border of the old Indian Territory, later to become the State of Oklahoma. This border town was rather rough. It was made notorious by drunken Indians, and by a famous bank robbery by the Dalton brothers and by the visits of Carrie Nation with her hatchet. Often I was awakened in the middle of the night by sounds of gun fights and by drunken brawls. Fortunately, we lived next door to the Episcopal Church and every time there was a service the McKinstry family was in the building dutifully saying their prayers. Perhaps this was a great safeguard in such a rough place.

By the time I was six or seven, my father decided

to make one more move. Fortunately for us we moved to the town of Chanute, some fifty miles to the north. It was a lovely place, renamed after Octave Chanute the financial backer of the Wright brothers, famous for their flying experiments at that time.

Grace Church, Chanute, housed a congregation of people who were fine and loyal but not too numerous. The church was located directly across the street from a huge Methodist church, and the contrast was rather dramatic. It was in tiny Grace Church that I received my greatest inspiration. My rector was the Reverend George F. Degen, a Boston aristocrat who, with his wife, Edith, had ventured forth from New England to try out the less settled Kansas life. His wife was the most fascinating person I had met to that time. She was related to the Noyes family of Newbury, Massachusetts. This was of great interest to me because the sister of my great-great grandfather, George McKinstry, had married Daniel Noyes in that same area, leaving us, no doubt, somewhat related.

I was the rector's only altar boy and I had a standing invitation to breakfast following the early communion service. These experiences were not only fun but full of rich wisdom.

The Degens made a deep impression on me and remained my dear friends until God removed them from this earthly existence. Many years later I presided when their remains were buried in a New England cemetery.

I attended the public schools in Chanute, Kansas, which I must admit, were not uniformly excellent, despite a few outstanding teachers in the high school. I was interrupted in my high school studies because of illness which forced me to take a year off for recuperation. When I finally graduated I was advised by my doctor not to go at once to college but to wait until my health improved still further. But I was sure I was on the road to complete recovery. Besides, I felt I was called to the ministry and I must be on my way.

I chose to go to Kenyon College in Gambier, Ohio. When I said good-bye to my parents at the railroad station in Chanute, my father reminded me that when I needed more money I should write home. However, I never needed to take him up on the offer. It all came about in this way.

At the end of my first week at Kenyon, I was summoned by the president of the college, Dr. William Foster Pierce, a very impressive gentleman, to talk with him in his office. I was petrified lest I had committed some terrible breach of ethics, or had broken some important rule of the college. I appeared before this august person, who, to my surprise, was most polite and gracious in asking me to be seated.

In a more relaxed state of mind, I heard him say that the college organist had left and that he had heard that I played a church organ. He wanted to know if I would be willing to apply for the post as college organist. I quickly and bashfully assured Dr. Pierce that I was not quite that good. But the president was persuasive. He asked me to try it out for a month and see how I liked it. I did, and I was college organist throughout my career there.

This past, coupled with my appointment as assistant at the college commons, made it possible for me to go through college without ever writing home for money, an unusual experience, which would be most unlikely to be duplicated today. I also had time for dramatics in college and each year I acted the role of Hamlet under the direction of the famous English professor, William Peters Reeves.

It was indeed providential that I chose Kenyon College because this college was one of the few institutions which still practiced freshman hazing. For example, we had compulsory chapel in those days each morning, except Saturday. And every morning at the end of my musical performances, I would line up with the other freshmen and, in lock step formation, march out on the campus no matter what the weather. We were ordered to kneel on the ground, often damp or snowy, and "boola, boola". This was the equivalent of a very vigorous setting up exercise. Then we were told our sins and ordered to make amends. At the end of this session, we were ordered to "cuckoo", which meant that we broke ranks and jumped in the air lustily shouting "cuckoo", flapping our wings, so to speak, rushing down the lengthy campus to the dormitories. This was a wonderful exercise, and what was presumably meant to haze me in fact caused me to flourish physically.

In my senior year I moved to Bexley Hall, the Divinity School of Kenyon College, and combined my last year at college with my first year in the seminary. It had always been an ambition of mine to go to Cambridge, Massachusetts, to study at the Episcopal Theological School there, and also at Harvard College. I had had great difficulty persuading my Bishop in Kansas, the Right Reverend James Wise, that this was a safe thing to do because he had heard that the Episcopal Theological School had many radicals—and possibly "low churchmen".

I must admit that many years before, one of the professors at Cambridge had taken a firm view in regard to church issues and churchmanship. The famous Dr. Steenstra on the Cambridge faculty in the 1880's had been lecturing one day to his class on pastoral care. He had cautioned the young students that they must always counsel parishioners in need of advice in the open church. He had said to them, "You must not go into a room and close the door, for instance, because that might sometimes lead to embarrassing situations."

By some hook or crook there was a student present in that ancient period in the school's life who advocated belief in auricular confession. So this protesting student, who had got into the seminary in some mysterious way, spoke up and said, "Well now, Doctor Steenstra, you say that we should never never receive a parishioner in a closed room or a place apart from people. Is this quite the way to hear auricular confession?"

At this, Dr. Steenstra exploded:

"Young man, this church does not practice auricular confession. Young man, you take my advice—"

The young man interrupted, "Well, just a minute, Doctor. The early church fathers practiced auricular confession."

Whereupon the professor, with his finger still suspended in mid-air, said, "Young man, I say again to you, take my advice, or some day you may wake up and find yourself an early church father."

Although Bishop Wise had not objected to the emphasis of the student who had argued with Dr. Steenstra, he was indeed afraid of the fact that the Episcopal Theological School would be too liberal in theology. It was with great reluctance that he finally gave his permission, and I went to Cambridge and to Harvard Graduate School, with great expectations and joy. Being at last in the land of my forefathers was really almost more than I could stand, and, excited and delighted every time I went out, I thought I could feel the presence of my colonial ancestors.

I might add another reason for my soul being delighted: my fiancee, Isabelle Van Dorn, daughter of a well-known Cleveland industrialist, who graduated from Harcourt School in Gambier, Ohio, about the time I left Kenyon, had obtained permission of her family to attend a school known as Rogers Hall, in Lowell, Massachusetts. Every Saturday evening I took the train from Boston to call on the young lady in Lowell, always taking her a box of candy. This weekly experience made my life in Cambridge even more exciting. Another highlight was my association with a man destined for considerable fame and influence at Harvard. I had as my tutor Harold J. Laski, a political scientist on loan from London University. Mr. Laski was a brilliant scholar and an eloquent lecturer.

Many years later he became head of the Labor Party of England. I wrote a thesis under Mr. Laski in the field of political science. I maintained my contacts with this interesting person over the years until he died.

On April 25, 1920, St. Mark's Day, I was ordained to the priesthood by Bishop Wise in Grace Cathedral, Topeka, Kansas. This quick trip back to Kansas towards the end of my experience in Cambridge, was a great moment for me. At long last I had been ordained as a presbyter, and also I was introduced on that occasion to the Cathedral congregation in Topeka as the canon-elect of its Cathedral.

Being graduated from seminary in 1920, I was ready to move out into the world and to begin my ministry.

Inasmuch as I had gone to Cambridge as an ordained deacon, I had been able to serve on the staff of the Cathedral Church of St. Paul on Boston's Tremont Street.

Dean Edmund S. Rousmaniere of St. Paul's was a remarkable person, a great mystic. He impressed me deeply by his emphasis on personal religion.

So now I was graduated and I left Cambridge on June 17, 1920 for Cleveland, where I married Isabelle Van Dorn two days later. The service took place at the summer estate of her family at Rocky River on the banks of Lake Erie. We had the service on the grounds there because one of her grandmothers was too ill to go to Immanuel Episcopal Church in the city. Immediately thereafter we left Cleveland on a honeymoon which soon ended in Topeka, Kansas, where I was installed as a canon of Grace Cathedral and chaplain of Bethany College, now defunct.

Chapter 4

Brink of Disaster

My experience at Grace Cathedral in Topeka nearly ended in disaster. The dean was the Very Reverend James P. deB. Kaye, an Englishman who had been at the cathedral for many years. He felt its design and construction to be his crowning achievement—and seemed to worship the glory of the cathedral next to the Almighty.

When I arrived I soon discovered Dean Kaye never did any parish calling. In fact, he sat in his office most of the time, scheming the next move that would keep him ahead of his critics in the congregation. He sought to avoid anything painful or harmful to his peace of mind.

Sensing that the congregation was woefully neglected, I requested him to let me do systematic parish calling. He said, "Of course, go ahead." He cautioned me on certain subjects that were to be avoided in my conversations with parishioners. Even so the people were extremely responsive to my visits.

Another thing that bothered me was the fact that this wonderful cathedral was locked up after Sunday morning services. Nothing took place in the edifice between Sundays, so I asked the dean for permission to hold Sunday night services. I told him I had just come from Boston where Dean Rousmaniere held successful Sunday night services. I explained that Dean Rousmaniere had preceded the service by hymn singing, first in front of the cathedral on the porch, and then, having begun the service, he would invite the crowds to come inside. The services were conducted in a very informal way, and the cathedral was crowded every Sunday night.

I explained I would add another feature by holding a social hour in the parish house prior to the evening service, inviting parishioners to bring their neighbors—and especially any prospective members of the Episcopal Church or any lapsed members.

Dean Kaye was sure the plan would fail. He said he would personally have nothing to do with it. He gave me reluctant permission to try, with the understanding he would not be involved in any way. I went to all of the cathedral organizations, explaining my plan and receiving their promises of cooperation and I augmented the choir of thirty-five by bringing in thirty more voices.

We were successful from the very beginning. People indicated a desire for parish social life, and the Guild Hall was crowded each Sunday evening. The organizations vied with one another to produce interesting but not elaborate refreshments. After developing a cordial atmosphere, we moved into the cathedral for the service itself. It was really quite inspiring. The morning services normally attracted perhaps 200 or 225 people each Sunday. But in the evening service we began with at least 400, and the number increased.

The dean came to the services too. He sat in the congregation, looking very unhappy. One day the senior warden came to me and said, "It doesn't look right for the dean to be out there in the congregation. Why don't you invite him up into the chancel?"

"Why, of course," I said. "I will be glad to."

So the dean came into the chancel the next Sunday night. He evidently expected to take over the service and preach. However, I fooled him. I did the preaching and let him read the Lessons. At the end of the season, the dean announced to me and to others that he had decided to close the Sunday night services in the cathedral. When I asked him why, he said they were too embarrassing. "You get so many more people than I do in the morning."

Needless to say, the news of all this got to the people and there was a rebellion. I was shocked to learn that a petition signed by hundreds of the congregation had been sent to the Bishop urging him to fire the dean and name me the dean. I had not expected anything like this. I went to the dean at once and told him how very sorry I was and, of course, he knew I had had nothing to do with the petition. He said he quite understood the situation but that it had gotten out of hand. He refused to change his mind about the Sunday night services.

At this particular time I had received a call from the Church of the Incarnation, Cleveland. Indeed, the call had come three times. So I went to Bishop Wise saying that things were too embarrassing at the cathedral, that I felt I had better resign. The Bishop agreed, believing, he said, that my leaving would put an end to the dean. He said he would like me to resign and put myself in his hands. I countered with the suggestion that since there were no vacancies in the diocese, I felt that this would be a dangerous thing to do. After all, I was married and we were expecting a baby. He then said he was thinking about sending me to a little Kansas oil town named Caney. He would rent a small empty store room on Main Street there and establish a mission. He said there were three or four communicants in the town and he thought he would like to send me down there to start a new work. He admitted that none of the people there had requested him to do such a thing.

I reported this development to the dean, who said, "If you go to Caney it will be like sending you to Siberia in the eyes of my congregation, and my usefulness here would be ended. My great ambition has been to live and die here and to be buried under the altar of this cathedral, which I built."

Back in my office I then wrote two letters, one declining the call to Cleveland, the other accepting it. I took these letters to the dean and said, "Now you tell me which one I should send."

He said, "I must say that I feel it would be happier for you and for me if you should go to Cleveland."

Therefore, I made the Bishop most unhappy, and upset a lot of people in the cathedral by moving much sooner than I had ever expected to. However, I had learned an important lesson in my dealings with the dean: an assistant must never outshine his boss.

Chapter 5

Cleveland to Albany

In Cleveland I inherited a parish which had been all but ruined by scandal in the family of the previous rector. It was my responsibility to rebuild and to persuade the parishioners who had wandered away to come back to the church. And this was not an easy thing to do.

I had followed a man who had been very handsome and proud, all six feet four of him. The scandal had caused many of his members to stay home on Sundays or to go elsewhere. Fortunately for this parson, his superior, the Bishop of Ohio, the Right Reverend Andrew A. Leonard, liked him and appointed him archdeacon of Ohio, a very important post.

I had begun my rectorship with some of the ideas I had learned from Dean Rousmaniere in St. Paul's, Boston. For one thing I immediately launched a systematic parish calling program. And I repeated the Sunday night service plan which had worked so well in Topeka. Lapsed members began coming back. Soon the church was filled to the doors and one morning the tall, handsome, proud archdeacon showed up in my office to ask about rumors that certain of his former flock had returned and were again worshipping in the church.

Suddenly he said to me, "You are trying to show me up. I can ruin you for this. I have the ear of the Bishop."

As a young man full of ideals, I was completely shocked. What could I say? The Lord gave me the answer.

"Archdeacon, when I came here I knew that I was following a 'big' man and that I would have to work very hard to fill your shoes. Now, if the lapsed members have been led to return to their church as the result of my ministry here, and I have only been trying to follow a 'big' man, then I would say that the results are due primarily to the inspiration of God the Holy Spirit. I suggest that you take this matter up with God if you wish to protest."

The archdeacon—or the "archdemon"—left, but he told other clergymen that he would reckon with me by influencing the Bishop against me. Secretly I doubted this. The Bishop had always been a very gracious friend of mine. He had baptized our first child.

In any event the archdeacon remained very unfriendly. Nonetheless, with the help of God and through considerable effort and sacrifice I led the congregation in building a handsome church.

My Cleveland experience introduced me to the strange world of finance. The first night I presided over the vestry after my arrival as rector, the treasurer of the parish informed the group that a considerable amount of money had come into his hands because Robbins and Myers, a company in Springfield, Ohio, had recently "called" in the bonds which were part of our building fund. He asked for instructions.

Immediately the clerk of the vestry, J. Edmund Flynn, first vice-president of the Cleveland Discount Company, a first mortgage company, said, "I move the money be invested in the bonds in my company." I thought the man was entirely too eager to get his hands on the money. Although I was not very old, twenty-four years of age, I did have enough sense to see through that.

So I asked as a courtesy to me, the new rector, the vestry let the matter rest on the table for one month. Mr. Flynn was quite ruffled at this and he said, "Why, your own father-in-law is a director of the company."

I said, "This may be, but it has nothing to do

with what I am asking. I am asking to be allowed to get my feet on the ground—we won't lose very much interest by tabling this thing for a month."

The vestry supported me. A week or so later the treasurer of the parish phoned me and said, "Did you know that Mr. Flynn has been circulating a resolution among the vestrymen authorizing him, between vestry meetings, to take the bond money and invest it in first mortgage bonds of the Cleveland Discount Company?"

At the next meeting of the vestry I said, "Don't you ever do a thing like this again." Mr. Flynn did not attend. I was very nervous about this. I had been in the Cleveland Discount Company Building, a handsome building on Superior Avenue. Quite often I would note that in the beautiful counting room there was not a soul on the floor representing the customer's side, but only the clicking of machines behind the cages.

So, being a little suspicious and anxious, I went to the treasurer of the company, a Mr. Peck, and explained that the money we had invested in their bonds was a part of our building fund, and we might need it any day. I asked him to give me a letter assuring us that he would redeem the bonds on sight.

One day, a broker friend, called me and said "Something is going to happen to the Cleveland Discount Company and I want you to get busy with those vestrymen and get the bonds out of hock, and into the hands of the treasurer of the Cleveland Discount Company immediately."

I called a vestry meeting. Mr. Flynn was not available. I got a resolution passed. The next morning I was on my way downtown with a vestryman to get the bonds out of the safe deposit box. The morning paper had announced the forced resignation of the president of the company. We called on the treasurer, taking his letter to me. While we were discussing the matter with him, my father-in-law, who was indeed a director and terribly anxious about the company, rushed into the office and said, "Mac, what are you doing here?" I showed him the treasurer's letter and said that we were there because we wanted our money for our building operations, not because of the news headlines.

Mr. Peck, immediately asked us to return at one o'clock and he would have a check for us. I was there as requested, and I received the check as promised. I took the check to the bank, had it certified, and deposited. Within three weeks the company blew-up.

My father-in-law's face was red. While he didn't lose any money, it came out in the courts that Josiah Kirby, the president of the company, had falsified his records and had lied to the board of directors. Mr. Kirby ended up in prison. I was always afraid someone would come after us and make us return the money, but no one did, and I think I can safely say that we were probably the only people to get our money out before the crash.

After the new church in Cleveland was completed, I received a call from the Presiding Bishop of the church inviting me to the National Council in New York, to serve as an officer in the Field Department. The Field Department was educational in its scope, but it was also the promotional arm of the general church. In this capacity I was asked to develop contacts in New England, especially in the Diocese of Connecticut.

I was also sent frequently to the deep south. This entailed a great deal of traveling, which did not please my wife. But by this time we were settled in a new home which we had built in Westfield, New Jersey, placing Isabelle near her favorite cousins, so she was not entirely without some family contacts during my absences.

As a result of my frequent preachments in Connecticut, I became friendly with the Right Reverend Chauncey B. Brewster, the diocesan Bishop, and his assistant, the Right Reverend Edward C. Acheson—father of the late Secretary of State, Dean Acheson. I had been ordered by headquarters to persuade the Bishops of Connecticut to hold annual clergy conferences. The purpose: to develop fellowship in the diocese, enlarge the missionary vision of the parsons and, ultimately, of their congregations. Annual clergy conferences were quite common in most dioceses but there had never been one in Connecticut. I succeeded in convincing the Bishops of the diocese that this would be a wise plan. They decided on place and date for the first conference the next September.

I then asked them whom they would like to have as their leader. First I offered them the Presiding Bishop of the church, then the national treasurer of the church, also Doctor John W. Wood, our "Secretary of State for Foreign Missions". To each one of my suggestions, they said, "No, thank you."

By this time I was getting a little worried. Then they completely shocked me by announcing that since I had convinced them of the worthiness of this plan, and had sold them on the idea of an annual clergy conference, they wanted me to be the leader. I was only twenty-seven years of age. The idea of talking to 200 rather sophisticated parsons in Connecticut was overwhelming.

I hied myself back to New York to the Church Missions House and reported these strange and highly embarrassing developments. However, my superiors agreed I should accept the assignment. I never worked harder on any address in my life. I worked on it all summer.

I arrived the day before the scheduled conference, checked into a hotel and worked on the remarks I planned to deliver.

The address took forty minutes. When I concluded and walked off the stage, the audience, 200 rather hard-boiled parsons, stood up and gave me an ovation. The Bishops sent for me to come back on the stage for a "curtain call". This had never happened to me before—and I guess, not since.

My experiences in the deep south were also very rewarding. Bishop Frederick F. Reese of Georgia invited me to visit his parishes and to address the people of his diocese on the missionary work of the church.

In this general work I became very well acquainted with the entire church, and with a great many of the clergy, along with many of the laity. Because of my youth, I had agreed to serve on the National Council staff for only a period of three years, or little over, believing that my true vocation was in the parish ministry.

Therefore, on February 1, 1927, I became the rector of St. Paul's Church in Albany, succeeding the Reverend Doctor Roelif H. Brooks, who, after twenty-five years as rector there, had become rector of St. Thomas' Episcopal Church in New York City. St. Paul's was possibly one of the largest churches in upper New York State. I was entirely responsible for the administration of this parish. I also was the vicar of a suburban mission which Doctor Brooks had founded in nearby Elsmere. At first I had no assistant. However, I did find time to do some diocesan work and to serve in community affairs. The Bishop of Albany appointed me chairman of his Department of Promotion. I also became chaplain of the New York State Legislature.

I might add that certain rectors had gone from St. Paul's into the episcopate in the years before. For example, the first Bishop of California, the Right Reverend William I. Kip, came from St. Paul's. Also the Right Reverend John Scarborough of New Jersey. The Right Reverend Alfred Harding of Washington had also been rector of this parish. Indeed, the Bishop Coadjutor of Southern Ohio, the Right Reverend Theodore Irving Reese, who had ordained me deacon in Trinity Church in Columbus, Ohio, had grown up in St. Paul's rectory at a time when his uncle, the Reverend Livingston Reese, had been the rector.

To be asked to serve a parish in the capital city

[34]

of New York State was a very interesting assignment since, if you were to believe those who lived there, Albany was second in importance only to Washington. It was said that sooner or later nearly every important person in America and abroad paid a visit to Albany.

Albany's old Dutch influence soon became apparent to me. It was, of course, prominent in colonial and revolutionary days. The city was very conservative. I often listened to tales of newcomers to Albany who complained about the coldness of the residents. It was almost impossible to get into the social life of the city, according to these stories, but, as rector of St. Paul's, I had ready entree to the social life and my wife and I found it, on the whole, very interesting, stimulating and exciting.

[35]

Chapter 6

"Two Minute Charley"

One of the characteristics of life in Albany, in my day, was the almost universal custom of "putting up" motor cars from December until April because of the intense cold and heavy snows. As late as May 1, thick ice would remain in the gutters in front of my rectory, and many people relied on taxis and chauffeur-driven black limousines—especially for weddings and funerals.

The Albany Motor Renting Company, two blocks from my rectory on Lancaster Street, had a supply of limousines and chauffeurs. The latter were somewhat coarse. I, quite by accident, discovered they had nicknames for many of the clergy of the city. They called one Baptist parson "Steamboat Sam", and another "Blood of the Lamb". I coaxed the chauffeurs to tell me why. Why, I wanted to know, did they call the Baptist minister with a Van Dyke "Steamboat Sam"? The answer: he always preached a sermon at funerals about a ship sailing from the harbor (of this life) into unknown seas. The climax was the final arrival of the good ship safely into the harbor of Heaven.

The parson called "Blood of the Lamb" generally preached a long funeral sermon about the cleansing blood of the lamb.

When I begged my informants to tell me what they called me, the chauffeurs balked. However, after much persuading they consented to reveal my nickname. They said, "When you came to the city we didn't know very much about your 'terminal' facilities. The first funeral we had at St. Paul's Church was in the dead of winter, a very cold day, and after getting the congregation nicely seated, we all went off to a speak-easy. We had expected you to last at least thirty minutes. But you fooled us. You lasted only fifteen minutes, and we got bawled out by our employers. So we call you 'Two Minute Charley'."

As it turned out, this was an altogether appropriate nickname for me. It took a "Two Minute Charley" to do all the things required of me as the rector of St. Paul's, and the vicar of St. Stephen's, Elsmere.

This was my Sunday schedule: at 8 a.m., I had the communion service at St. Paul's. At 9 a.m., I had a similar service at the suburban parish, St. Stephen's. At 9:45 a.m., I rushed back to open the church school service at St. Paul's, after which I taught a class of boys. At 11 a.m., I conducted morning prayer and preached. At 3 p.m., I opened the church school at St. Stephen's, and, at 4 p.m., I read evening prayer and preached. By 6 p.m. I was back at St. Paul's to meet with the Young People's Fellowship. And, at 8 p.m. Sunday, I conducted evening service and preached again.

During the week I carried on systematic calling, by appointment, on the people of the parish. I divided the parish into zones for calling purposes. Fortunately, I was a young man then, and I was able to get along at first without an assistant. Then along came the Reverend C. H. Leyfield, who had been a pastor of the large North Avenue Methodist Church in Baltimore. We prepared him for the ministry and he was ordained. A second assistant came later on, the Reverend Howard Farnsworth.

Bishop Philip Cook of Delaware, whom I had met at summer conferences, used to call on me at St. Paul's. He was greatly annoyed at me for being in what he called a "soft" parish.

I couldn't see anything soft about it. It was a well endowed parish. It did have some of the city's finest people on its rolls. But he thought I was much too young to be in such a plush post. He suggested I ought to be out in the west, doing a hard missionary job; but I could see nothing wrong with my parish. It was a tough job, and it was a position which I very much enjoyed. So I politely told him so.

As chaplain of the New York Legislature, it was my duty to open the sessions with prayer. Before the 1930 opening the papers had carried a back-page reference to the possibility of a march on Albany by "Reds". No one paid very much attention, chiefly because nothing like it had ever happened before. So one morning I mounted the granite rostrum in the great chamber to offer morning prayer—a prayer for the unemployed of the country.

Before I began I noticed something very unusual. Every gallery of the vast chamber was packed to

suffocation. The rear of the chamber was also crowded. I could almost smell danger. I showed the presiding officer the text of my prayer and added that intuition told me the prayer might possibly touch off a riot. We both agreed that the people in the galleries and the rear of the chamber were indeed strange looking. I put the prayer in my pocket and decided to offer one for the general direction of the legislature. I left the rostrum, went down to the floor and began shaking hands with a few of the legislators. The clerk had begun to drone out the minutes of the day before.

At a given signal, the galleries in the rear of the chamber were alive with shrieking, shouting, cursing humanity. Men and women screamed and shook their clenched fists. The members of the legislature stood up in amazement at such an exhibition. Looking at the stone rostrum where I had been a few moments ago, I could see that the visitors had grabbed one of the capitol guards and were dangling him head first over the rail ready to release him. If they had he would have been killed instantly.

A riot call had gone out, and the state police, in great numbers, rushed into the chamber. They rescued the capitol guard who was about to be killed amidst a kind of pandemonium I have never seen before or since. On that morning, I learned how it felt to be angry enough to kill.

The state troopers and guards were finally able to rout the unwelcome visitors, from the galleries and from the back of the chamber. Whether they were communists or just trouble-makers I do not know, but it was the first time a thing of this kind had happened in this country. It was so horrible I have never forgotten it.

Early in 1968, when I recited the story to Rabbi Herbert Drooz, of Temple Beth Emeth in Wilmington, who had been a teenager in Albany at the time, he told me he had a vivid recollection of the riot and that his uncle was a legislator at the time.

When I moved to Albany, Alfred E. Smith was the Governor. But he soon decided to try for the Presidency, and wanted Franklin Delano Roosevelt to run for Governor of New York, believing he would most surely be elected. At that time the Democrats of New York were meeting in Syracuse, and Governor Smith announced to his intimate friends there his plans for inveigling Roosevelt to run for Governor. He had Eleanor Roosevelt, who was present at the convention, call her husband and plead with him to accept the nomination.

[39]

But Eleanor did not get very far. Governor Smith tried his hand at it—also John J. Raskob. But Mr. Roosevelt was quite stubborn on this point. He said he was out of public life and was an invalid. He felt he had to stay in Warm Springs, Georgia and minister to his ills. I was told that Mr. Raskob asked one question, "How much do you owe at Warm Springs?"

At any rate, Mr. Roosevelt was persuaded to run. He was elected Governor of New York and Alfred E. Smith was defeated for the Presidency.

I remember the first dinner given for the Roosevelts after their coming to Albany. It was at the

Dewitt Clinton Hotel and several hundred people were present. Governor Roosevelt came into the room leaning heavily on the arm of an aide and using a cane with his right hand. People had dreaded the moment of his entrance, feeling great pity for the poor invalid. But for all his physical problems FDR was about the most attractive, charming human being I'd ever seen. Very soon people were entirely persuaded that his crippled condition would not interfere with the effectiveness of his work. I have seen him enter the Governor's Mansion leaning on his aide and using a cane, and at once grabbing a pair of crutches and flying around the room to shake hands with each of the guests.

Albany society, which had felt particularly cheated during the Smith regime, rejoiced that aristocracy had returned to the Governor's Mansion. They waited hopefully for the first high tea to be given by Mrs. Roosevelt. But Mrs. Roosevelt, not sensing this, and being interested in a school and a furniture factory in New York City would be absent from Albany virtually the whole week, returning only for the weekend.

Soon Albany society became very discouraged about the prospects of any activity in the Mansion House. A good friend went to Mrs. Roosevelt and explained the situation to her, whereupon the Governor's wife sent out engraved invitations, with one going to the rector of St. Paul's Church and his wife. We all gathered expectantly at the Mansion. I remember how Mr. Roosevelt came in— how gracefully he moved among the guests on his crutches. But what almost ruined relations between the Mansion and the society of Albany was the fact that on that occasion Mrs. Roosevelt served only bouillon cubes and saltine crackers. Albany society felt cheated again.

Before Governor Smith left office, and since I was at the time chaplain of the legislature, it was my personal honor to say the dedicatory prayers on the day the Saratoga Battlefield was declared a national historic site.

Governor Smith was always very careful to be quite proper. And although he was guilty of mispronouncing certain words, such as "raddio" for "radio", he was a wonderful person and a great leader. After the dedication of the Saratoga Battlefield, important people were invited to his room in an old hotel. While they remained in his room everything was exceedingly dignified. But when the last of the "proper" Albanians and Bostonians had left the room, the Governor took off his coat and, peering around at the rest of us, said, "Friends." From under the bed he pulled suitcases full of suitable libations.

After five years on the Albany scene, I was called to be rector of St. Mark's Church, in San Antonio. This call was accepted only because I became convinced that God wished me to go. The truth of the matter is that I didn't want to go at all. And my dear wife wept every mile between Albany and Texas.

Chapter 7

St. Mark's—
The Cradle of Bishops

The people of St. Mark's Church in San Antonio have been, and still are, proud of their church's history. In 1931, when I became their rector, there was much talk about how it had served to launch three Bishops.

There was Philip Cook of St. Mark's, who had become the fourth Bishop of Delaware. W. Bertram Stevens had gone from St. Mark's to the bishopric of Los Angeles, and S. Arthur Houston to be Bishop of Olympia, Washington. (Since then, four other rectors have been elevated to Bishops.) It was indeed a wonderful parish but, for all of God's prompting, my heart remained in Albany. Despite the fact that Bishop Cook used to poke fun at me for being in what he called a "soft" place, like Jonah of old, I just didn't want to go to "Nineveh". But in the end, Jonah, too, knew that God had truly called him to Nineveh.

When my call to San Antonio came I thought if I could not altogether ignore it I could at least not pray about it. This was really hiding from God. However, the Presiding Bishop of the church at that time, the Right Reverend James DeWolf Perry, sent for me to come from my comfortable parish in Albany to see him and his fellow National Council officers in New York. They argued with me that I ought to go to San Antonio. They wanted me to reorganize the Diocese of West Texas because it was too desirous of having the national church's subsidy increased.

It was explained that Texas was beginning to boom. They pointed out that across an imaginary line, in the mother Diocese of Texas, centered in Houston, the church was growing by leaps and bounds, while in contradiction, the church in west Texas was weaker than it had been in years. I was exhorted to accept the call to St. Mark's and do what I could to get Bishop Capers and his people to realize that a new day was dawning for Texas.

Also, they reminded me that San Antonio was a great military center full of young men in training who deserved a better place in which to live.

I had little notion of the implications of all of this, but later I found that in the year 1931 San Antonio had the highest mortality rate from tuberculosis and enteritis, a baby's disease, of any city in the United States. The city also had a notorious vice district, and much corruption was suspected in the halls of the municipality.

I went home from my conference with the National Council officers and began, at long last, to pray about my call. And in every moment of prayer I could hear God's voice saying to me, "Go down to San Antonio."

Thus, I meekly accepted, despite the anguish caused by my wife's bitter tears.

We arrived in a seven-passenger car with a driver, and I was wearing a derby hat. Nobody wears a derby in Texas and I got rid of the hat and the driver as well. We were soon adapted and in the midst of a whirlwind experience. Bishop Cook had gotten his way. He had finally dislodged me from a comfortable, nice place, much to the bewilderment of the congregation in Albany. The senior warden of St. Paul's in Albany, Sydney Tucker Jones, in his farewell words to me said, "We had expected you to remain here for perhaps twenty-five years, then, like your predecessor, Doctor Brooks, go to New York to one of the big parishes such as St. Thomas' or St. Bartholomew's. And to think that you are going to Texas!"

Soon after I arrived in San Antonio, I was almost immediately plunged into community affairs. I was early elected a member of the board of directors of San Antonio's Chamber of Commerce and, mysteriously, I was appointed chairman of the Public Health Committee. The appointment enabled me to observe the vice and corruption at first hand, while remembering the large number of young men who were serving at Fort Sam Houston and the various flying fields on the outskirts of the city. These young men had been trustingly committed to San Antonio by their families back home.

It was shocking to find the older and more responsible citizens of the city took the prevailing vice and health conditions pretty much for granted. I was told, "It has always been like this, and it is due very largely to the Mexican population." However, I was unwilling to let these matters stand unchallenged, so I appointed a very strong Public Health Committee. It was composed of a noted physician, who had a real public concern and a Jesuit priest, Father Trancasey, who packed a lot of influence among the Roman Catholics, especially the Mexican population. I also had the assistance of a young broker, Elmer Ditmar.

Our committee soon invited the American Social Hygiene Association to come to the city and use their secret operators in a survey of the vice conditions in San Antonio. We also asked the United States Public Health Service to conduct a secret survey of general health conditions and to recommend a more effective use of the Department of Health in and around the city.

Then I persuaded twenty-five leading businessmen of San Antonio to meet with me secretly once a week to study the problems of the city. This they agreed to do, providing I would not reveal their identities. They were that afraid of the loss of city business. One of these men was Walter McAllister, a banker, who was extremely helpful to me. He and others of the secret group actually became so involved and enthusiastic they became members of what has been known ever since as the Better Government Movement, which prevails to this day. Indeed, Mr. McAllister, who much later became mayor of San Antonio, and others who succeeded him, were adept promoters of their city. The Great World's Fair of 1968, held in San Antonio, came about largely due to Mr. McAllister's leadership.

In my time it seemed necessary to get the city machine out of office. We proceeded to do just that, electing Maury Maverick, son of a famous Texas family, to be the first mayor under the new regime. We were also able to snatch the public school system from the grasping hands of the old regime, which had desired to control it. We put our own hand-picked Board of Education into office through the means of the ballot. This board then engaged Thomas Portwood as superintendent of schools, and he served in that capacity for many years with great distinction. Under his leadership and planning, San Antonio schools moved to the head of the procession. He and his board provided for school integration long before other major cities had even begun to think about it.

During all of those exciting and hectic years of struggle with policitians, I had taken great pains not to neglect my work in the parish. I felt it to be wise not to make the issues of the city subjects for my sermons. I never made a single speech about these conditions, or preached a sermon about them. I knew the quickest way to kill a movement was to shoot the leader dead. So I depended on others to do the speaking. We had a very excellent speaker's bureau which covered the city and every civic organization which would listen. We had excellent cooperation from the newspapers. Indeed, we had the public with us in the emerging campaign to clean-up San Antonio and to bring in good government. But even so, my tasks had proved to be most difficult and dangerous.

One evening I received a telephone call from a *Time Magazine* correspondent, who was staying at the St. Anthony Hotel and he asked me to come down to see him on important business. When I called on him, he told me that *Time* had assigned him the responsibility of covering our fight for better public health conditions in the city. He spoke of the secret U. S. Public Health survey. He said he had seen a copy of this document but that the public health people in Washington had overlooked one important factor, they had not learned that there was leprosy in the city of San Antonio.

I said, "How do you know about that?"

"We have absolute proof of it," he said, adding that he had written an article for *Time* covering the fight we had made, including everything about the surveys and the leprosy. He was mailing it to his editor that night for publication the next Tuesday.

I objected. He said he had a photograph of me, and was writing the article around me and my leadership. I vigorously protested, pointing out it was not fair for him to do this because many people were involved. I could see myself being ridden out of town on a rail; even the businessmen who had stood by me would point the finger of scorn at one who had ruined the tourist business via the leprosy item in an issue of *Time Magazine*.

I tried to convince the correspondent it was wrong, under the circumstances, for him to submit his article, but he was adamant.

I went home very much shaken. The next morning I went to the office of Bolivar Clegg, a prominent businessman and a friend of the mayor. The mayor had stubbornly refused to cooperate with our health committee and with the Bexar County Medical Association, in the effort to have a better run health department. One of the sections in the *Time* story dealt with the mayor's refusal to throw out of office the ward heelers who held key jobs in the health department of the city. I told Mr. Clegg about my interview with the *Time* correspondent, about the leprosy angle and the fact the article would go to print the next Tuesday. I said I wanted him to tell the mayor that if this article came out he would be finished politically.

I also asked him to tell the mayor that if he would meet with my committee at three o'clock that afternoon and agree to sign the plan for the re-organization of the public health department of the city, I felt I had enough influence to persuade *Time Magazine* to kill the article.

My fellow Rotarian Mr. Clegg grabbed his hat and rushed off to the mayor's office with the news that I had imparted to him. Within an hour he telephoned me that the mayor was terribly frightened, and would meet with my committee at three o'clock that afternoon, and also sign the plan for re-organization of the public health department.

[47]

Then I phoned Mr. Luce of *Time Magazine*. I congratulated him on his concern for the city of San Antonio. I also congratulated him on the article, which had been prepared, but I begged him not to publish it. I explained, at length, that the mayor had finally capitulated and would cooperate with the Public Health Committee in accomplishing the things for which we had been fighting. I thought the mayor should be given a chance. . . and the article killed. If it appeared it would undo all the good which had been accomplished by his correspondent.

Mr. Luce was most gracious and said that in view of the fact that many young men in the military would be involved, with their lives much improved by the developing plan, he would kill the article. But he added, "Tell the mayor that if he double-crosses you, we will still publish the article." I passed this information on to the honorable mayor—and with great pleasure. My scalp had been saved!

It was only a matter of time before the mayor and his machine were thrown out of office and we had a fine new mayor in Maury Maverick.

Chapter 8

Two Presidents and I

Two rather important events took place during my life in San Antonio. The first was a call for me to be rector of St. Thomas' Episcopal Church, Du Pont Circle, Washington, D.C., in 1935.

This call, I learned, had been suggested to the vestry by one of the communicants, President Franklin Delano Roosevelt. He had known me quite well during my rectorship at St. Paul's, Albany, and we had kept in touch. Apparently he had decided I was the man he wished to succeed the retiring Dr. Thomas Smith. The President wrote me as follows:

Dear Dr. McKinstry:

When you come to Washington to consider my parish I want you to visit me at the White House because I have some definite ideas as to how that parish should be run.

Very sincerely yours,

Franklin D. Roosevelt.

I went to Washington to look over the church. I visited its beautiful rectory. I preached in the Cathedral in Washington, and I, of course, listened to the President. But I returned to San Antonio and, in my sermon at St. Mark's the next Sunday (when I faced an Easter-size congregation, which had learned I had conferred with President Roosevelt, who was extremely popular in San Antonio) I announced I had received a call to St. Thomas' Church, Washington. However, I told them, I also had another call—a request from the people of my parish to stay on as rector, since I still had many more things to accomplish.

The matter did not end there. Soon the call to go to Washington was extended to me for the second time. I declined once more. A third call came at the insistence of the President. By then I was half annoyed but certainly impressed. I telephoned Bishop Cook in Wilmington, and asked him, "Is this a call from God?" He roared back, "No—stay where you are." So once again I declined.

About six months later, FDR came to San Antonio to dedicate a public building. He arrived in his special car at the Southern Pacific depot. When he walked slowly down the ramp leading from the car to the sidewalk, I was a member of the committee of twenty-five that had gathered to greet him.

As he moved down the ramp, holding the arm of his aide, he suddenly spied me some distance away and stopped. He transferred his cane to his left arm, raised his finger and, in a shrill voice, cried, "McKinstry—you were a wicked man! Why didn't you come to Washington and be my rector when I needed you?"

[50]

I, of course, felt a little embarrassed, but I wasn't too annoyed by this. I did admire the quickness of his mind. I knew perfectly well he hadn't thought of me on his way down, but seeing me instantly set into motion a chain reaction.

James A. Farley was with him on this trip and he was quite irritated. He had arranged for me to sit on his right at the luncheon following the dedication and he played up to me in a very gracious way. He later sent me a beautiful letter, which I often wish I had kept. As I said, I was not annoyed at Roosevelt, I was simply amazed at his ability to remember such things—and by his gift of instant recall.

The other event occurred on the 7th of November, 1934, a day I went to my office as usual at nine o'clock. A telephone call came to me from Postmaster Dan Quill of San Antonio. He said that he had a young man named Johnson from Washington, Secretary to Congressman Kleberg of the King Ranch family, who desired to be married by me in St. Mark's Church.

I asked, "When?"

Mr. Quill amazed me by saying, "Why, this evening, at 6 p.m."

I explained that holy matrimony was a very serious and important matter. I needed time to talk to the young couple before I was prepared to perform the ceremony.

But Dan Quill made a most impassioned plea. He said, "This young man is in a hurry. He has to get back to Washington. There is no reason why you can't marry them legally. I'll never do this to you again, but they want to be married in your church this evening at 6 p.m. Please do this for me."

In a sense, I was against doing it but I agreed because of the circumstances, and the promise Dan Quill would never put me in such a position again. [51]

So, at six o'clock, I met the young couple and agreed to perform the ceremony in the church. There was no music. There were no flowers on the altar. There were only the bride and the groom, their witnesses and two or three other people, including Dan Quill, and a Jewish lawyer named Hertzberg.

As I was about to begin the ceremony the young lady, Lady Bird, spoke up and said, "Lyndon, dear, you did think to buy a wedding ring, didn't you?"

Lyndon exploded, "Gee—plumb forgot the ring."

I gave Dan Quill a dirty look. He grabbed his hat, shouting, "The jewelry stores are all closed now but Sears Roebuck is open."

He rushed out, clambered into his car and soon

was back with ten assorted sizes of $1.50 wedding rings. He had promised to return those not used. We proceeded with the ceremony.

At the conclusion, and after the newly married couple had moved aside to do their embracing, I whispered to Dan Quill, "I doubt that this marriage will ever last."

It did, though. The couple became known throughout the world as being most devoted. They never forgot me. When Lyndon Baines Johnson was inaugurated as Vice-President, along with President John F. Kennedy, the Johnsons saw to it that Mrs. McKinstry and I were invited. We went from our home in Easton, where we were living at the time. We enjoyed ourselves enormously.

Often we were invited to state dinners at the White House. In the living room of my apartment, I have many autographed photographs of the Johnsons and their family. In my files are many letters from both the President and Lady Bird. I have been to the LBJ Ranch. I cherish my continued contacts with Mrs. Johnson. Before the Johnsons left the White House, she invited me there for a last visit, and I took along with me Mrs. Richard C. du Pont and her rector, the Reverend James O. Reynolds.

In 1974, Mrs. McKinstry and I returned to Washington to be Lady Bird's guests at a great party, at which we attended the first showing of a new documentary on the life of Lyndon Johnson.

To return to San Antonio: It was obvious that God was charting a new course for me. Mrs. McKinstry and I had become thoroughly at home in San Antonio. We had become very much a part of the general community.

St. Mark's Church was indeed wonderful, but after nearly eight years there, I received a call from Christ Church in Nashville, Tennessee. This came in the fateful

[52]

For Reverend and Mrs. Arthur R. McKinstry
who have known the Johnson family from the
very beginning — with our best regards
Lady Bird Johnson   Lyndon B. Johnson

year of 1938. Trouble was brewing in Europe and an international explosion was about to rock the world.

It was with considerably heavy hearts that the McKinstry family once more pulled-up stakes and settled in Nashville in August of 1938.

Christ Church was a noted parish, and once more I heard the stories of how many rectors had become Bishops. But being a Bishop was far from my thoughts as we became part of the city and the Christ Church parish. Five of my immediate predecessors there had entered the House of Bishops. The two rectors preceeding my arrival were the Bishop of Tennessee, the Right Reverend James M. Maxon, and his Coadjutor, the Right Reverend Edmund P. Dendridge.

My schedule at Nashville, was extremely heavy. First, I begged off from the usual stuffy reception accorded by parishioners to the incoming cleric and his wife, substituting for that orthodox practice fifty smaller neighborhood receptions to be held in the homes of parishioners. This latter plan had necessitated holding two home meetings each night, five nights a week, during the fall season. This proved to be a most rewarding experience for the new rector, and, I might add, a mighty shot in the arm for parishioners, active, occasional or inactive.

At each meeting, or little reception, I gave a brief prepared talk about the parish plans for the future, and urged all present to attend Sunday services. I would have individual chats with those who attended, and I tried desperately to memorize names and faces. The hostess, at these meetings, would invite the guests into the dining room to confront tables loaded with the kind of refreshments for which Nashville people are famous.

Some 700 people attended these neighborhood meetings, whereas the traditional receptions, held in the downtown parish house, attracted a possibly 200 of the faithful and regular communicants. The immediate boost in church attendance was a tangible result of this unorthodox plan. Also, it gave the members of the parish an opportunity for some parish social life, as well as a chance to look over the rector.

Another reason for my being busier than usual was the fact that I had lured the vestry of Christ Church into doing a wholesale job of repainting and refurbishing the old and rather dreary parish house. I persuaded the vestry to have the classrooms and public rooms of the parish house adequately lighted, and was given authorization for a modern office set-up. My first three months were lived at a terrific pace. All this fails to chronicle the responsibilities of the rector and his wife for guiding our five children to new and strange schools—a project of no small dimension.

By mid-November, the new rector was able to look back upon almost three months of feverish activity with some relief and no little sense of satisfaction. It was now time to take a day off and motor the family through the lovely Tennessee countryside. We went to the University of the South at Sewanee, which is located on "the mountain", seventy miles from Nashville, where the beloved University of the South has a campus of 10,000 acres.

[55]

My knowledge of Sewanee and the University of the South located there, had been considerably limited up until about 1935 when I had come from San Antonio to receive an honorary degree. Through the years I had known many dear friends who were ardent Sewanee boosters. The Reverend R. Bland Mitchell, always became sentimental with the mere mention of the name Sewanee. I first knew Doctor Mitchell when he was executive secretary of the Field Department of the old National Council of the Episcopal Church located in New York City. I had been chosen by him and the Presiding Bishop to be his associate.

My experience with Dr. Mitchell had put me

into intimate touch with Sewanee men, many of whom were Bishops and leading clergy of the church. And much as I loved and admired them all I'd become a bit prejudiced against Sewanee. They all raved so much about it. I thought no college could be that wonderful. Besides, as a graduate of Kenyon in Ohio—also of the Harvard Graduate School and the Episcopal Theological School in Cambridge, Massachusetts—I had my own ideas of how great a school could be.

So it was with some skepticism that I visited Sewanee in June, 1935, to receive an honorary degree and to preach the commencement sermon. However, something occurred during that commencement which inspired me. Doctor Ben Finney, the beloved vice-chancellor of the university for many years, had announced his retirement, effective after the commencement exercises. The news of this had been a source of disappointment but seemingly accepted as final. On Saturday, two days before Commencement, Mrs. McKinstry and I were at lunch at the vice-chancellor's home. Suddenly there was a knock at the front door. Doctor Finney went to answer. We heard voices outside the house, then silence, and when Doctor Finney did not return to the table, his niece, Mrs. Johnson, my wife and I went to investigate.

We saw a long column of college students walking toward the college chapel and Doctor Finney was at the head of the procession. Bells were ringing everywhere. People were gathering from all directions—white and black, civilian and collegiate, old and young.

I recognized a friend and asked him the cause of the commotion. He told me that the students had just learned that the trustees that morning had persuaded Doctor Finney to remain another academic year. Overjoyed, the students had routed out the college chaplain for a great service of thanksgiving in the chapel. My mind went to my own college in Ohio, and I wondered if such an occasion had arisen at Kenyon

College would the students have instinctively felt that the chapel was the proper place of rejoicing. In any case the chapel at Sewanee was crowded with faculty, students, townspeople, workmen and servants, and it was one of the most moving experiences of my life.

And so on that day, after I had witnessed the strength of the religious program at Sewanee, I decided that when my son, Jim, went to college I would try to use my influence to have him admitted to the University of the South. And that is exactly what he did do some years later.

(After several semesters he entered the Navy during the war years. Upon completing his tour of duty with the Navy, he did not return to Sewanee. He went instead to Washington and Lee, because it offered courses not available at Sewanee which would prepare him for a law degree.

However, I wish to emphasize again that my first Sewanee commencement made me a real rooter for this college, with its strong and unashamed church traditions and loyalties, and I remain today an ardent Sewanee supporter.)

It was natural, when we moved to Tennessee that I would want my children to go to Sewanee to see the beauty of the buildings and campus. Mrs. McKinstry also looked forward to a return visit. So on November 15, 1938, we all crowded into our car and were off on a great lark. The country was beautiful. We had an inspiring time at Sewanee and returned late in the evening to our rectory in Nashville.

The minute we entered the rectory, the phone began to ring.

It was to be the most important telephone call in years, and its ringing shattered thoughts of a delightful life I had anticipated in Nashville. It also rang-in a new era for the McKinstry family.

Chapter 9

The Reluctant Bishop-Elect

I answered. Western Union was calling.

A telegram had come from the presiding officer of a special Delaware convention which had met that day in Wilmington to elect a new Bishop. The message informed me I had been elected the fifth Bishop of Delaware. In quick succession came other telegrams, including one from the Bishop of New York, the Right Reverend William T. Manning, a former rector of Christ Church, Nashville, urging me to accept my election and inviting me to come to New York to discuss the matter with him.

I had known Bishop Manning quite well when I was a young rector St. Paul's, Albany. My first impression of the Lord Bishop of New York had been exceedingly negative. This was due to his refusal to allow an inter-denominational communion service in Grace Church on lower Broadway. The rector of that church had asked the Bishop's permission to allow the Reverend Doctor Henry Sloan Coffin, a famous Presbyterian parson in New York, to participate in the service of Holy Communion.

This, of course, was before the ecumenical movement had been envisioned. The New York newspapers had made a big and ugly story of the Bishop's refusal. I felt certain that I would never like him.

At the age of thirty-one I had actually preached a sermon in St. Paul's Church, Albany, denouncing Bishop Manning for what I thought was ineptitude and lack of vision in his handling of that inter-denominational communion service.

However, a year or two later when the organist of St. Paul's Church, Dr. T. F. H. Candlyn, and I took our famed boy's choir to New York to tour St. John the Divine, which was in process of being built, Bishop Manning, standing at his office window, spied us on the grounds. He told his secretary to cancel his appointments. He came down and joined us, introduced himself and insisted on taking us on a personally conducted tour. He was so gracious we all loved him on the spot. And having been elected to his former parish, Christ Church, Nashville, I very much wanted to consult him about my problems.

In addition to the message from Bishop Manning, I of course received a telegram that day from the chairman of the election committee of the special convention, which had been held in Immanuel Church, Wilmington. It was signed by the late rector of St. Anne's Church, Middletown, the Reverend Percy L. Donaghay. It read:

> We have the honor and pleasure of advising you that you have been unanimously elected Bishop of Delaware at a special convention in Wilmington today. Kindly advise your convenience in receiving our committee of notification.

There was also a telegram from Colonel George A. Elliott, prominent Delaware layman, saying:

> We are all very happy at being able to elect an old friend of Bishop Cook without politics or bitterness.

I also find in my file many other congratulatory telegrams and letters from prominent clergymen and laymen all over the country.

A re-reading of these documents is a humbling and inspiring experience for me personally. Most of these messages urged me to accept the election, if I felt I had been called. A few who knew the Nashville situation pointed out that my associate rector at Christ Church, "Father McCloud", had been the continuing pastoral minister through five previous rectorships. All of these men had in turn been elected Bishop of some diocese.

However, at the moment I received notification of my election, I was completely bewildered. In a moment of desperation, I telephoned Bishop William T. Capers of San Antonio, my former Bishop, shouting to him, "Bishop, the most terrible thing has happened to me."

"What is that, Mac?"

I replied excitedly, "I have been elected the Bishop of Delaware."

I heard a laugh at the other end of the line.

"What's so awful about that?"

I then weakly tried to explain I did not see how I could possibly leave a very challenging work which had been so recently begun. Bishop Capers tried to calm me down, saying, "Sleep on it, Mac."

So that day, which had begun so innocently and peacefully, ended in a nightmare. The rector of Christ Church slept very little that fateful night.

After lots of publicity in the Nashville papers, the church, on Sunday, was crowded with curious people to hear what I had to say. I told them that all my sympathies lay with Christ Church and that I hoped they would leave me alone to wrestle with my problem; that it would take several weeks to come to a definite decision. The people of Christ Church cooperated wonderfully. They are that kind of people.

I knew so little about Delaware and the diocese. Of course, I had known the Right Reverend Philip Cook, the fourth Bishop of Delaware, who served as Bishop from 1920 through most of 1937. I had always loved him; indeed he was my son Arthur St. Clair's godfather. His death had been a great shock to me. Naturally I knew

Colonel George A. Elliott, Sr.

Mrs. Cook and their children. I had also met Colonel
Elliott and his wife in Kennebunkport, Maine, where they
had a summer cottage and I was in charge of St. Anne's,
for several summers. I knew a former rector of St.
Andrew's Church in the 1920's, the Reverend Doctor
Richard W. Trapnell. He had asked me to preach at St.
Andrew's in the autumn of 1925. But I had no other
contacts with the Diocese of Delaware. I needed to know
more about the church, the state—something about future
opportunities of the church, before I could adequately
weigh every aspect of my call. Besides, I had to feel sure I
had been truly called.

For this reason, it was decided I would meet the
committee of notification representing the diocese in New
York City, rather than allow them to come to Nashville.
Consequently, within a week Mrs. McKinstry and I went
to New York. I met the committee at the Hotel Chatham. I
recall some of the members: The Reverend Percy L. Don-
aghay, the Reverend Charles F. Penniman, the Reverend
R. K. White, E. W. Maynard, MacMillan Hoopes, Judge
Richard S. Rodney and, of course, Colonel George A.
Elliott.

We had a very frank discussion about the diocese. I asked the committee what kind of a Bishop they
needed in Delaware at that time. This produced a long and
at times a warm discussion. I recall that Mr. Maynard
bluntly stated that what the diocese needed most was a
greatly improved lot of clergy. Obviously, this did not
please the parsons who were present.

I liked all the men very much. Since the diocese
had held two conventions for the purpose of electing a
successor to Bishop Cook and each time the Reverend
Doctor Charles W. Clash, rector of Immanuel Church in
Wilmington, had been nominated and each time had
failed to be elected, I asked the committee if they felt he
would seek election for the third time if I should decline
my election. The members assured me that would not

[62]

happen under any circumstances. They also said that Doctor Clash was a fine, loyal rector and would be most cooperative.

At the first special convention in Delaware, the Reverend Doctor Oliver J. Hart, then rector of St. John's Church, Washington, had been elected but had declined for various reasons. Doctor Clash had been the candiate in that convention's competition. Sometime later, Doctor Hart was elected Bishop of Pennsylvania. At the second convention, I had been elected over Doctor Clash. The fact that he had been nominated twice speaks of the high regard he was held by many of the people of the diocese.

It was manifest to me that the delegates of the convention had expressed the desire to have someone from outside the state, to serve as Bishop at that particular time.

One of my reasons for going to New York was to see both the Bishop of New York and the Presiding Bishop, and receive their ideas about Delaware and my election. Bishop Manning couldn't have been more affectionate. He had prayers in his office, and as a former rector of Christ Church, Nashville, he urged me to accept, saying he knew something about Delaware and he thought the diocese could move forward. He counselled me to avoid feeling sorry for the people of Christ Church, Nashville, reminding me of the wonderful associate rector, "Father McCloud".

Both Bishop Manning and Bishop Tucker, the latter a cousin of Bishop Dendridge, my immediate predecessor, emphasized the fact that McCloud was the beloved pastor of the Christ Church congregation. Both men strongly urged me to accept my election if I could feel the call.

After our meetings in New York, Mrs. McKinstry and I boarded the Pennsylvania Railroad train for Wilmington where we were entertained at dinner by Colonel and Mrs. George A. Elliott at their home. I recall some of the guests: Mr. and Mrs. Henry F. du Pont; Mr. and Mrs. Walter J. Laird; Mr. and Mrs. Irving Warner; Mr. and Mrs. Ernest N. May; Mr. and Mrs. Howard Seaman and others.

The following day, I called on some of the Wilmington churches to meet anyone who seemed inclined to talk to me. I learned much about the past. It was not clear to me how much my informants realized the needs of their diocese for the immediate future. Obviously the diocese was not very active at the time, for there had been no Bishop since 1937.

The late Bishop Cook had been greatly interested in foreign and domestic missionary programs of the church. For several years he had served as president of our National Council in New York. This necessitated his absence from the diocese a great deal of the time. He did a lot of traveling and he had to preside at meetings of the general church. It was necessary for him, of course, to return to Delaware on weekends to meet with his congregations—to carry on visitations and confirm the flock. During his absences he had to rely on the Reverend Charles A. Rantz, then the rector of the Church of the Ascension, Claymont, whom he had appointed executive secretary of the diocese for the daily administration of the affairs of the Executive Council.

After learning all we could about Wilmington and about Delaware, my wife and I returned to our home in Nashville. It was time to try and find our way through a maze of uncertainties. What was my duty? Could I feel God's presence and know His will and direction in this matter? Naturally, I was willing to do anything consistent with God's plan.

Did not the psalmist of old write? "Where there are no changes—the people fear not God." I realized the people of my parish were attempting very hard to leave me alone to struggle with my own problem. Only once did a member of the church show signs of forcing the issue.

He suggested a special meeting of the vestry and the parish council. A remarkable layman named Vernon Tupper, violently disagreed by saying, "Let the rector alone till he feels that he knows God's will."

So, I was allowed to take my own time. I do not want to over-dramatize the experience but I can say sincerely that night after night I prayed for guidance and, frankly, seemed to get none.

Then on a Sunday night I had two callers: The Right Reverend R. Bland Mitchell, the Bishop of Arkansas, and a very distinguished clergyman from Trinity Church, Houston, the Reverend Thomas N. Carruthers. Both men had been to Sewanee for a meeting of the board of regents and were en route to their respective homes.

These two very dear friends had come to find out what I had decided, reminding me that of which I was painfully aware—that I should send the Diocese of Delaware my decision very shortly. My friends could easily see I was weary and worn, having slept poorly for two weeks. I told them I thought I would probably have to decline my election.

Bishop Mitchell got up and began to pace back and forth in my study. Finally he blurted out, "Mac, if you were still the rector of St. Mark's Church, San Antonio, and you had this decision before you, tell me honestly: how would you feel about it?"

Rather surprised, I said, "Why . . . in that case, having noted the opportunity in Delaware, I rather think I would accept the election."

Both men were now standing and shouting in unison, "Then you must accept now; you are just feeling sorry for the people of Christ Church."

This, they said, was entirely unnecessary, considering the ministry of McCloud. I was startled by their confrontation. After they had gone I decided I would retire for the night. I went into a front room, determined to pray the whole night long, if necessary. I had to have an answer to send to Delaware. I had tried for weeks to get some sort of an answer to my prayers and had received none.

After an hour of meditation and prayer I had one of the most remarkable spiritual experiences. The word came through to me very clearly that I was to accept the election. Feeling completely at peace for the first time in over two weeks, I slept soundly the rest of the night.

The next morning, Mr. Tupper telephoned at seven o'clock to ask me to come to his office as early as possible. I arrived at 8 a.m. He was anxious to tell me he too had been praying consistently that I might know the right decision. He said the previous night he had prayed again and he got the message very clearly it was my duty to accept the election.

I was quite amazed that he cared that much to really pray seriously for me. I explained what had happened to me. He jumped from his chair and said, "That settles it. Let's get Charley Martin (the senior warden) on the telephone and ask him to call a special meeting of the vestry and the men's council for this very night."

That evening forty-eight men assembled. Vernon Tupper spoke first, describing his personal experience the previous night. Then I told of my own experience and decision, although I admitted my sadness over the thought of leaving Christ Church.

The senior warden, Mr. Martin, then addressed me and the men saying, "Do not blame yourself. We were warned when we called you as rector of Christ Church that this might happen." He never explained how he knew and I never asked. "We called you just the same," he said. "And if we had to do it all over again we would call you again, because you have more than justified our wisdom. You have launched us on a very much-needed program here, and the parish is prospering."

Then Mr. Martin added, "Now we want you to name your successor."

I was aghast at this. I explained to him, and the men, that I shouldn't do this. It was never done. It would be most unwise. But they insisted. Then I said, "Well, I readily nominate the Reverend Doctor Thomas N. Carruthers of Houston, Texas."

They informed me he had been the man they had in mind to call in case I declined their call. I was asked to talk with Doctor Carruthers by telephone, inviting him to come to Nashville immediately for a conference.

Doctor Carruthers, agreed to come. After a conference with the vestry he accepted the call. He moved to Christ Church shortly after my departure and continued the program I had begun, although he amplified it in many areas. He did such effective work that in five years he was elected the Bishop of South Carolina. He was a very fine preacher, a truly godly man, beloved and respected by all. His early death in South Carolina was a great tragedy for the whole church.

[67]

With the feeling that we were leaving Nashville most reluctantly, but with the goodwill of many of the people of that community, we departed on our eventual trip north. Because we had three weeks between leaving Nashville, and the day of consecration in Delaware, we decided to visit Florida for the first time and call on my wife's father, Thomas Burton Van Dorn.

Before leaving Nashville, I wired my father-in-law, who was wintering on his yacht at Fort Lauderdale, that we planned to pay him a visit. He bluntly replied,

Do not come—difficult to find accommodations here.

I laughed at this and told my wife that we would find some place to stay and without any further warning to him, we started for Florida.

In due time we got to Miami, going first down the west coast of Florida and over the Everglades Trail. We went to Hollywood, where we stopped at the Seville Courts, a motel where one of my Nashville families was staying. I told my friends what Mr. Van Dorn had said in his warning and that we were a little bit nervous as to whether we would find a place to stay in Fort Lauderdale for a week. My Nashville parishioners then advised me to meet Lee W. Moffitt, the owner of the motel. He was a wonderfully kind Kentucky gentleman. When he heard our story he said, "I have the answer to your problem. Follow me."

He took us up to a new home in Fort Lauderdale on one of those fascinating canals off Los Olas Drive, not far from the beach: He and his wife had not yet lived in this house but it was completely furnished with everything new. Mr. Moffitt said, "This is yours for as long as you want it."

Being a Scotsman, I said, "How much?"

He told me not to bother about that until we were ready to leave Fort Lauderdale. Incidentally, he charged us the ridiculous price of $1 per person per day; mother, father and five children. What is even more important, the Moffitts became our very close friends. Many years later I officiated at Lee's funeral in Tennessee. Mrs. Moffitt still lives in Hollywood, Florida.

After we were nicely settled in the new house, we called on my father-in-law on his yacht. When he saw us coming, he fairly shouted, "You won't find a decent place to stay here."

We assured we were comfortable in a lovely new home on one of the canals near Fort Lauderdale Beach. He looked confused and baffled—almost angry. He did come to dinner that night however, and was amazed. Later he wrote the family in Cleveland, "Darndest people I ever saw—always land on their feet."

After a fine rest we were ready for Wilmington—a strange and unfamiliar place to us all. Not knowing how long the trip north would take I refrained from specifically naming the day of our arrival in Wilmington. I rather vaguely wrote we would arrive sometime around February 12th or 13th. I thought that when we got to

Wilmington we would first rest and in due time notify the people of Delaware we had arrived.

We arrived safely and soon were settled in Bishopstead—ready for the great day, the consecration of the next Bishop of Delaware in St. John's Cathedral, located at Market Street and Concord Avenue.

Chapter 10

"Pontifex Maximus" Mac

My personal diary for my first year in Delaware, reveals that I was a very busy person. I was constantly up and down the length of Delaware, visiting parishes and missions—often unannounced—meeting clergy and laity and forming opinions about my job and its assets and liabilities.

I had been greatly helped in my understanding of Delaware by Miss Elizabeth Lightner, who had served as Bishop Cook's secretary almost throughout his episcopate. One of the leading Wilmington rectors had urged me at the very outset to replace Miss Lightner with a younger and perhaps more efficient secretary. It was true Miss Lightner did not know shorthand. She was a bit lacking in "polite" talk, meaning that she usually called a spade a spade, regardless of whom she offended. Her salary was $100 per month, and, in addition to being the Bishop's secretary, she was the assistant treasurer of the diocese.

I felt that anyone whose work had satisfied Bishop Cook was good enough for me. Besides, she had a vast amount of information about the diocese and the people of Delaware. I needed to know all she could tell me about my new work. Miss Lightner was used to Bishop Cook's absences from Wilmington because of his many years as president of the National Council in New York. She was quite experienced, therefore, in covering for the Bishop and in running the office without his presence. This was a great asset, because she could now use her techniques in my behalf while I was out of the office roaming the diocese, forming my own impressions for future programming.

From the very first day, I had loved quaint little Delaware. It was unlike anything I had ever known. And I liked the people. It is not to disparage anyone to say that the state's lower countries were unspoiled and unsophisticated, and, I must say, a bit isolated in those days—an isolation the people enjoyed.

In 1939 no one had ever thought of building the Delaware Memorial Bridge, or the Chesapeake Bay Bridge, or the bridge-tunnel at the tip of the Delmarva Peninsula. All of lower Delaware, and indeed the entire Delmarva Peninsula, was somewhat cut off from the mainstream of contiguous United States. This seemed to bother not a soul living there.

Downstate Delaware was most charming, with a sort of "let the rest of the world roll by" attitude. My conversations with Sussex County people revealed a sense of pride in their state of affairs. Obviously, when anyone wanted to go abroad or to go on trips in this country, he had only to drive to Wilmington, where he would find the Pennsylvania Railroad station, or highways like Route 1 or Route 40 or Route 202. And yet, I felt that the church life and organization—as lovely and quaint and wonderful as Delaware was—were some years behind the standards in the church generally.

I realized that the people of lower Delaware, being proud people, were also rather sensitive and at times resentful towards Wilmington and New Castle County. I was a bit surprised to find some of the leading churchmen in Sussex extremely critical of members of the Du Pont family, for example, when actually they knew very few of them personally.

The farmers up and down the state had bitterly resisted T. Coleman du Pont when he told them he wanted to buy some of their land between Wilmington and Dover. His plan was to build, and subsequently give to the state, a fine dual highway—probably the first in the country at that time. Downstate people were extremely suspicious of Mr. du Pont, since they couldn't imagine anyone being that generous. They felt he must have some ulterior motive in all this, and so they fought him bitterly when he tried to buy land on which to construct the highway.

Of course, he succeeded ultimately in his project and I think what resulted made a deep impression on the people of the whole state. After the highway's construction, I feel sure, the attitude of suspicion on the part of the people of southern Delaware was much less noticeable. The key to the whole matter was, as always, simply better communication.

I could clearly see that in my role as Bishop I had to be working behind the scenes. In fact, I had to build spiritual bridges of understanding between lower and upper state people. I have always been fascinated with the history of bridge building. As a matter of fact, bridge building—the bridging of streams—is rather modern. For example, the word "bridge" does not appear in the Bible. The explanation is easy: there were no bridges. In ancient times men were stubbornly opposed to the idea of building bridges. Why?

First, people didn't trust their neighbors. They had gone many times to peer across natural boundaries or streams at their neighbors on the other side and, since they weren't quite certain as to whether they represented danger, they were very happy to have streams and other barriers separating them from those across the way.

There was still another reason why the streams were not bridged in early times: the fear of river gods. For centuries, people believed superstitiously that streams were presided over and governed by little gods. They feared that if they tried to bridge the stream the river gods would become angry and would have an excuse for flooding the terrain.

It is interesting to note that in the Middle Ages the church decided to do something to eliminate man's silly objection to bridge building. The Bishop of Rome borrowed a title from the Caesars. He called himself Pontifex Maximus. In Rome's heyday there had been an order of bridge builders, over which the Caesars had presided. Julius Caesar had the title of Pontifex Maximus, the chief bridge builder.

In those days, however, the Latin word "pons" did not refer to bridges of stone or wood. The term had to do with spiritual meaning. The Roman order of bridge builders existed to keep the channels between the gods and man open. However, after the Roman Empire became Christian, the Pope had another, more practical idea. He organized orders of bridge builders whose mission would be to build bridges of stone and wood across the streams. He was determined to overcome man's silly ideas and prejudices, and he was determined also to develop understanding among people.

The Pope even granted indulgences to those who helped with bridge building and so, little by little, bridges became the accepted thing, uniting tribes and people, even nations in Europe. Indeed, the bridges of Europe signalled the true beginning of communication, the beginning of commerce.

Coming to Delaware and finding that people in Sussex and Kent Counties were actually suspicious of some people in New Castle County, and realizing that this was a frequently unjustified feeling built up through generations, I was determined that one of my jobs was to serve as a modest Pontifex Maximus, doing what I could to bridge the gaps between lower and upper Delaware.

I recently consulted with businessmen in Wilmington who, in 1939, were responsible for the policy of the Delaware Chamber of Commerce. I asked them what their experience had been at that time in regard to a lack of unity in the business world of the state. A very responsible and knowledgeable individual told me that he had made the same observation that I had. He agreed that it was not until the building of the Du Pont company's nylon plant in Seaford that the door was opened. Little by little, the subsequent years have evinced a better understanding between all sections of the state.

I realize that even as late as the 1960's the suspicion of which I have been speaking was not entirely non-existent. It still exists to some extent today. For example, within recent times, the Wilmington Free Library requested help from the state's divestiture fund for the improvement of the Wilmington Library on the grounds that it is a state-wide cultural establishment. A prominent official in Dover reacted violently to the proposal, saying to the effect that "If you people in Wilmington want to increase the size of your library, raise your own money up there."

I think this is an unconscious reflection of the thing I have been writing about. I don't believe it is as serious now as it used to be, but there is still work to be done. Bridges of understanding and trust still need to be completed even in this First State of Delaware. This can be done by the Bishop of Delaware and his fellow clergymen.

Therefore, long before engineers began plans for the Delaware Memorial Bridge or the Chesapeake Bay Bridge, my pastoral duty was very clear. The future growth and unity of the diocese demanded mutual trust and cooperation on the part of all people and we would need a unified program. We had to have enthusiastic support for that program. But this was not an easy thing to accomplish.

I had better give one illustration out of context. About one year after coming to Delaware I had quite a number of important projects going; a new church here, a new church house there—things that needed to be done, the beginnings of a program. One day in Georgetown,

Sussex County, I met a very important churchman on the street. This wonderful man said to me, "Bishop, you are using money to stir things up and to get a program started in this diocese, and I am delighted to see all this. However, I want to ask you one question. Is any of the money you are spending coming from members of the Du Pont family?"

The inference was very plain to me, and rather shocking. It revealed a situation that had existed for some time. With as much diplomacy as I could muster, I explained to my friend and fellow churchman, that the money came from special diocesan funds and endowments allocated for use by the Bishop of Delaware was now being spent by me—as rapidly and as wisely as I could spend it. The money had been unused in recent years by Bishop Cook because of his absence from the diocese and because of his busy work for the general church.

Well, the Sussex County churchman was visibly relieved. That encounter convinced me that, as Bishop, I must be a spiritual bridge builder. I must introduce some downstate people to fine churchmen upstate, and vice versa. By this procedure I must arouse a desire and enthusiasm of all churchmen in Delaware and galvanize their intelligent and sacrificial support for a forward-looking diocesan program, a program which would transcend parochial lines and which would be built and supported by all sections of the state.

By this time I was convinced that some kind of diocesan publicity program must be immediately planned and carried out, in order to inform the people and to give them some objectives toward which to work.

With this in mind, I went to Philadelphia to visit John F. Arndt, the son of a Germantown rector who'd been an old college friend of mine, John Arndt was a committed churchman himself, and the head of a large advertising firm to boot. His firm designed an attractive brochure, which projected a new program for the diocese. And this without any cost to me or to the diocese, though, of course, we did pay for the printing.

I personally distributed bundles of these brochures, going from congregation to congregation throughout the diocese, explaining to the clergy and the key laymen the importance of getting copies into the hands of their people. I'll admit that, thanks to my running around like a newsboy, the prestige of the office of Bishop of Delaware was somewhat lessened. Nor can I say that the dignified and sometimes complacent people of the diocese clapped their hands wildly when these printed works of art first appeared; indeed, I got a few nasty criticisms. But I was sure we were on the right track, and we carried on hopefully and with enthusiasm. In due time I was indeed rewarded.

Mr. and Mrs. Irenee du Pont were giving a coming-out party for two of Mrs. Philip Cook's daughters. Mrs. McKinstry and I arrived a bit early before the receiving line was set up. Mr. du Pont greeted me warmly and asked to speak to me privately.

"Bishop," he said, "I have been reading your brochures, in which you project a new program for the diocese, and I rather gathered it is your intention to develop the church in the State of Delaware."

I replied gratefully, "Mr. du Pont, this is the reason I came to Delaware."

"Good," he said. "You can count on me one hundred per cent."

Can any reader doubt for a moment that Mr. du Pont's enthusiastic endorsement of the Bishop's efforts meant something? As a matter of fact, up to that moment I had heard very little endorsement from anyone. Many people were kind and polite, but even the leading laymen, so-called, of the diocese were hiding in the bushes, looking over the new and strange Bishop, slowly making up their minds, wondering whether he was for real or just a flash in the pan.

Mr. and Mrs. Irenee duPont

Mr. and Mrs. Irenee du Pont never let me down. Once during a recital at Granogue by the ancient musical instrument artists of Philadelphia, Mrs. du Pont, that glorious saint and extraordinary mystic, took advantage of an intermission to take me aside. Her eyes were full of excitement, and she said, "Irenee tells me that I will have some funds to give away before the end of the year. Do you need any money for anything, Bishop?"

I was so startled I was really unable to say anything except to pour out my thanks. I promised her I would think about this and would send her a letter that would list projects which might be of interest to her.

In my Bishopstead study, I did a lot of thinking about this. How much did she have in mind? $100? $1,000? $5,000? How much? I had not the slightest notion. So I listed painstakingly and described about twenty projects ranging in cost from a few hundred dollars to several thousands of dollars each. I sent Mrs. du Pont the letter and told her if she did not find anything in my long list which appealed to her to let me know and I would try again. Weeks went by and I concluded that the whole matter had been forgotten.

Then, on the last Sunday in the year, after I had returned home from my Sunday appointment in Wilmington, I looked out my study window and saw Mrs. du Pont coming down the icy driveway at old Bishopstead accompanied by two of her lovely daughters. They were laughing and in great spirits as they tried to avoid falling on the ice.

They burst into Bishopstead with true Christian gaiety and happiness. Mrs. du Pont said teasingly, "You thought I had forgotten about your letter, didn't you?"

She handed me an envelope which I put in my pocket. I sensed somehow that she was slightly disappointed that I had not looked at the contents, so I asked her politely, "Shall I open the envelope?"

"Of course," she said. "There is nothing personal in this; in fact, I am only trying to be a good Christian steward. The money has been entrusted to me by God."

I have never forgotten that statement or her attitude on that occasion.

When I opened the envelope in the presence of everybody I nearly fainted. It was a check large enough to cover the entire list of twenty or more items, many thousands of dollars. Nothing like this had ever happened to me before. In the months and years that followed, whenever I found the going rather tough and needed some pump-priming, I was often at Granogue at an hour when I felt sure Mr. du Pont would be present. I would tell the two good people what I had in mind. Invariably, after a few questions, Mr. du Pont would say between puffs on his pipe, "Irene, you have some funds to give away. I think you should give the Bishop some help. Do you want me to take care of this for you?"

She would thank him and so would I.

Little by little, things were getting into high gear. Believing in the old adage "inform the mind and awaken the conscience", I early launched a Delaware edition of the National Council Magazine, which was then called "Forth". I made a deal with the publicity department of the National Council whereby we would have an insert of eight pages in each monthly edition of "Forth". By this scheme we would get a copy of "Delaware Forth" into each home in the diocese each month. It contained vital news and information about the diocese and its happenings, as well as projections of things to come. I progressively presented the new program to the diocese as we went along. Also, each copy of "Forth" contained interesting facts and information about the missionary work of the general church in this country and abroad. I knew that such information was desperately needed at that time, since I suspected that a great many members of the diocese were quite in the dark about the diocese and the general church as they went about their sacred duties.

Chapter 11

A Pastor for Clergymen

There had been no Bishop of the Delaware Diocese since the death of the Right Reverend Philip Cook in the fall of 1937. When I assumed the post, my contacts with the parishes soon revealed that the diocese had suffered because of this lack of episcopal supervision and pastoral care.

For example, in one prominent Wilmington parish I found a feud raging between the vestry and the rector. The spokesmen for the vestry were naturally the junior and senior wardens who came to Bishopstead to acquaint me with the details of their difficulties. They felt that unless these troubles could be eradicated the parish might ultimately be destroyed.

I listened very carefully to them. Then I met with the rector alone. It would serve no good purpose for me to discuss here the sad details of that story. Suffice to say I consulted with the rector's doctors, made my own investigations here and elsewhere and as I did, it became obvious to me the rector was really ill. He needed a change. Therefore, I proposed that the vestry offer him two years' salary in advance, something no one had heard of doing in those times. I suggested that he and his family go elsewhere to eliminate tensions. This would enable the rector to make a new start under competent medical advice. He accepted this very graciously and in due time he resigned and succeeded in finding more suitable work.

The friends of the rector had taken special note

of the known tensions between the wardens and rector. I suggested to the wardens it would be a statesmanlike thing for them to retire in favor of new wardens. Fortunately they agreed with my proposal. Very soon two other fine men were elected to replace them. This dissolved the tensions and a very important parish was saved. Since that day years ago, under very competent rectors, that parish has flourished, making a truly great contribution to the City of Wilmington, the diocese and the general church.

About that time, the senior warden of another important parish came to call on me with apologies for bothering me so early in my episcopate. He stated I would have to relieve their parish of its rector. They just couldn't "take him", he said, and he gave his reasons. Within a day or two, the rector himself came to see me and told me he would welcome any help I could give him in finding a new parish. He told me his reasons for thinking this, and they amounted to the fact that his congregation just would not accept his interpretation of the social gospel.

The next Sunday, I worshipped at that church's eleven o'clock service, and I listened very carefully. On Monday, I asked the rector to visit with me, and I recommended that he employ a fine voice coach, that he "perform a miracle" by preaching sermons lasting fifteen minutes and that he choose texts for his sermons.

I further suggested the rector call on his people more frequently and more systematically. I said, "If you do this, you'll have a very happy ministry." I told him I did not feel he should desert his post, or run away from his troubles, but rather he should conquer them and improve the quality of his ministry. He was capable of doing all this.

The rector looked rather startled and surprised. As he left my office, I hadn't the slightest idea of what would happen. Within a week, I encountered the parson's wife in a supermarket. She rushed up to me, exclaiming, "What have you done to my husband?" She went on to say she had never seen him so happy. Well, that fine man remained with his church for many years and performed a superior work, the greatest of his rectorship.

During my first year as Bishop, I also experienced two instances in which there was serious difficulty between a rector and his wife. I was compelled to take a hand for the sake of the people involved, as well as for the preservation of the congregation. In both cases, reconciliation, according to psychiatrists, was out of the question. Both men in due time resigned. In one case, I was able to secure work for the man in another diocese. In the years since, these congregations have gone from strength to strength in each instance have flourished.

There was still another parson who turned up hopelessly in debt and addicted to begging money from well-to-do churchmen, as a means of solving his financial problems. The churchmen being imposed upon had gotten weary of this sort of thing. I could see that some pastoral effort was required.

I requested the man come to me and bring all his bills. When he and his wife called, I talked to them about these obligations. He presented his list to me, but I had my own secret list which I had compiled with the help of others. Much to his surprise I produced some that he had omitted. I told him that I would pay all the bills, which together amounted to thousands to dollars. Then I asked for his resignation. I advised him that he had greatly damaged his ministry and that he would have to find another place. After my counselling, both the rector and his wife seemed sincerely anxious to make a new start. I am happy to report that I found the man a new parish in another diocese, where the situation was explained to the Bishop. The clergyman made a new start and subsequently did very well.

I cite these cases merely to show that, in 1939, pastoral work was much needed in Delaware, largely because there had been a rather long vacancy in the office of the Bishop. Morever, the incidents underscore a plain truth: a bishop must be pastor to all.

Chapter 12

My Friendship with the Laity

My pastoral ministry was not limited to the clergy alone. Shortly after I began my new ministry, I was informed I should be careful to observe limitations in regards to past "feuds" in the area. I soon learned all about the famous court trial between Pierre S. du Pont, Irenee du Pont, Lammot du Pont and their opponent, Alfred I. du Pont. This issue involved the disposition of the common stock of the Du Pont Company, which had been owned by T. Coleman du Pont and which was to be sold. The law suit split the family and caused bad feelings for many years.

It was tactfully suggested that as Bishop it would be well to avoid any contacts with Mrs. Jessie Ball du Pont, the widow of Alfred I. du Pont. I commented to my wife: "I have come here to bury feuds, not to prolong them."

So after Mrs. du Pont had come to Bishopstead to call on us, we returned the call and soon found her most charming and extremely interesting. We were frequently invited to her wonderful dinner parties, probably among the most brilliant in the Wilmington community. We would often find at her table such people as England's Duchess of Northumberland, who was the mistress of the Queen's robes; Sir James Purvis Stewart, the leading urologist in Great Britain; James F. Byrnes, former Supreme Court Justice and Secretary of State, and Mrs. Byrnes; Mr. and Mrs. Pat Murphy, he having once been Secretary of War; the first publisher of the "New

Mrs. Alfred I. duPont

Yorker" and similar luminaries, including members of her own family and Delaware friends.

Whenever I'd give a luncheon or a dinner in honor of distinguished guests, I took pleasure in seeing to it that Mrs. du Pont would be there.

On one occasion I gave a luncheon for the Right Reverend Henry St. George Tucker, Bishop of Virginia and Presiding Bishop, and my classmate the Right Reverend Henry W. Hobson, Bishop of Southern Ohio. I invited Mrs. du Pont.

At the door following the luncheon, she asked me if I would bring my guests to her home, Nemours, for tea. Both Bishops, Tucker and Hobson, said they would be delighted. As we passed the great gates leading up the avenue to her magnificent home I turned to my guests and said, "Do you expect to find tea?"

When I explained they would have their choice of spirits, each said in unison, "I never drink."

So when we were nicely seated in the library, the butler brought in all of the things I had predicted. With the greatest of self-assurance, Mrs. du Pont turned to Bishop Tucker, "Now, my dear Bishop Tucker, what may I serve you?"

St. George Tucker had noticed some small bottles of soda water on the tray and said, "Mrs. du Pont, if you don't mind I'll have a little soda water on ice."

Mrs. du Pont gave me a quick look, as much as to say, "What have I done?"

But he got his soda water on ice. Then she turned and said, "Now, Bishop Hobson, what may I serve you?"

"Ma'am, if you don't mind, I'll have a little soda water on ice."

She looked at me with despair, seemingly certain she had done the wrong thing. Completely upset, she turned to me and said, "Now, my own Bishop, what may I serve you?"

I replied that I would have whatever she was going to have. With a look of relief, she said, "I'm going to have some scotch and water."

"Make mine weak and I'll join you," I responded. I would have done almost anything within reason to relieve her embarrassment.

After a very pleasant conversation, when my

guests and I were leaving, Mrs. du Pont tugged at my coattails and asked if I could come to her office in the Delaware Trust Building the next morning at eleven-thirty. I agreed.

When I called, she chatted about how nice it was to have had Bishop Tucker and Bishop Hobson in her home. Then she turned to me and said, "Now, Bishop, you have always been so very considerate of me. Here is an envelope I want you to take. I am sure you have many projects in the diocese that require funds."

When I returned to my office, and opened the envelope I was simply amazed. The next time I wrote to my fellow Bishops, Tucker and Hobson, I said "Gentlemen, I must say that was the most profitable, weak scotch drink I ever had."

When the Reverend William C. Munds came to serve as rector for Christ Church in Christiana Hundred, I asked him to cooperate with me in eliminating some of the prejudices that had developed as the result of the law suit between the three Du Pont brothers and Alfred I. du Pont. He was of tremendous help, and very shortly I noticed that Mrs. du Pont was being invited to luncheons and dinners, and having a wonderful time. She was a really remarkable Christian.

In view of all the wonderful things she did for college students and institutions of learning and art museums, I felt she belonged in the American edition of "Who's Who". I appealed to the editors, with whom I had contacts since my own inclusion at age thirty-five, and I presented the case in behalf of Mrs. du Pont. The editors assured me they would welcome material supporting my nomination.

The next issue included Jessie Ball du Pont. She was delighted.

Some time later, I wrote to Doctor Alex Guerry, the vice chancellor of the University of the South suggesting that Mrs. du Pont be awarded an honorary degree.

Aside from her prominence, she had contributed much to the education of young people who could not afford college, and it might be fitting for the University of the South to recognize her in this way.

Doctor Guerry was responsive to my suggestion. He asked me to present substantiating material. I induced Mrs. du Pont's private secretary, Miss Mary Shaw, to work secretly with me in the preparations of the nomination. Mrs. du Pont was awarded the honorary degree of Doctor of Humane Letters. Mrs. McKinstry and I were invited to accompany her on the train to Sewanee the next June, her first visit to the University of the South.

I recall that the Bishop of Washington, the Right Reverend Angus Dun, also received an honorary degree at that commencement. Mrs. du Pont was deeply moved by what she saw at the University of the South. She began to ask questions about the financial needs of the college, and as a result she gave something like $7 million to the university over the years. This started a chain reaction among southern universities and colleges. Ultimately she received some ten or twelve honorary degrees. She had college buildings named for her, including the chapel at Rollins College. Over a period of time she must have given at least $25 million to southern colleges and universities. And I am very proud that I had something to do with this, since I was the first one to nominate her for an honorary degree, and I am pleased it was the University of the South which granted it.

Another opportunity for pastoral care was presented to me when MacMillan Hoopes, one of the trustees of the diocese and junior warden of Christ Church, asked me to go with him to meet his boss, Lammot du Pont, then president of the Du Pont Company.

We walked into Mr. du Pont's office, finding him seated at his big roll-top desk and smoking his pipe. Mr. Hoopes said, "Lammot, I would like you to meet our new Bishop."

Mr. du Pont didn't get up to shake hands with

me. He looked at me and smiled. He said, "Bishop, I think I had better declare myself. I do not believe in organized religion. I do not believe in the church." Mr. Hoopes was obviously perturbed over this unexpected development.

I said, "Mr. du Pont, what do you believe?"

He then went on to say he thought that every man should try to live a Christian life in all of his contacts with people, and to try and influence people for the better, and that was all there was to it. He said there was no need of organized religion, no need of the church.

By this time, I thought Mr. Hoopes would have a nervous breakdown. I am sure he was saying to himself, "This could be the finish of our new Bishop."

I said, "Mr. du Pont, I know you are a wonderful man. You are a very logical man and you have convictions. I appreciate your frankness and your honesty."

Then I went on to say to him, "When you close down your desk tonight, I hope you will lock it and not come back tomorrow. I would like you to meet me at the railroad station and take the Congressional to Washington."

Mr. du Pont despised Washington and when I said we should "go and call on the Commander-in-Chief, Franklin D. Roosevelt, and tell him we have a way to lick Hitler" Mr. du Pont looked a bit confused.

I quickly added, "Following the logic of your argument, I think we should request FDR to disband the Army, the Navy, the Marine Corps, the Air Force and every organized arm we have. All he needs to do is to furnish each American with a gun and turn him loose on his own. How far would we get, Mr. du Pont, in dealing with Hitler?"

Then I went ahead to point out to a rather surprised man that in my opinion, evil is the most powerful and highly organized entity with which we have to deal. Therefore, the need of strategy, the need of organization, the need of a program and the need of a church.

Mr. du Pont stood up. He shook my hand, gave

me the sweetest kind of smile and said, "Bishop you're right—I hadn't thought of it in that way. Good luck."

So ended a very interesting session. Often I would see him in Christ Church when I was there for some special occasion.

In due time he came to the end of his tour of duty as president and was retired. He still had many important responsibilities for the company. One day he telephoned my office, asking me to call on him the next morning at eight-thirty. I did so.

Mr. du Pont said to me, "Bishop, I hear that our diocese is booming."

I replied that I felt it was.

"I'm glad to hear it. Do you need any money for anything?"

I was taken aback, and since I couldn't think of a thing to say I told him he had caught me somewhat unprepared.

After overcoming my surprise I said, "I do have real need. Quite a number of young men serving in the armed forces have felt the call to the sacred ministry of the church. Some of these men are married, and it is very expensive for me to keep them in seminary. I could use some money for that."

"Good," said Mr. du Pont. "How much can you use for the next academic year?"

I figured quickly and told him how much I thought it would cost. He made a note of it.

"Now," he said, "don't stay away so long. Come around more often."

In a day or two I received a beautiful note from him and a check covering the amount we had discussed. Only a few months later, Mr. du Pont died.

I tell this story because I think it is a very sweet story. I had great affection for the man, also a great admiration for him.

I've mentioned earlier that one day in 1940,

while at Georgetown, Delaware, I was confronted by a leading churchman of that county who demanded to know whether any of the money I was using in a developing diocesan program had come from members of the Du Pont family.

This same man was a delegate to our General Convention in 1949. He was a very good friend of mine by this time. After the first session of the House of Deputies, he came back to the hotel where we were all staying and was very much upset.

He said, "Bishop, a terrible thing has just happened. Sitting right behind us in the delegation from the Diocese of Albany, and their dean is a rather nosy person. I overheard him asking Bob Downs, one of our delegates, whether he lived in Wilmington and whether he knew any members of the Du Pont family. I heard Mr. Downs say, 'Yes, I know members of the Du Pont family.' Well the dean said, 'Tell me honestly, Mr. Downs, are they good decent people?' Then Bob Downs said jokingly, 'Heavens, no. They are all atheists.'"

My fellow churchman and delegate to the convention from Sussex County was so upset about this he said something had to be done right away. He considered it to be a slur against the Du Pont family when Robert N. Downs III, could joke about such a thing. He demanded that I see Mr. Downs immediately and have him go to the dean of Albany and explain he was only joking because he himself was a member of the Du Pont family by marriage. When I told Bob Downs about all this, he was very much amused and immediately carried out the order I gave him.

I tell this simply because this same man nine years before seemed to be extremely critical of the Du Pont family, and now he was fighting for the maintenance of their high reputation in a distant city. This was the result of bridge-building in Delaware.

Another pastoral opportunity arose pertaining

to A. Felix du Pont, Sr. The first time I ever heard of this churchman was in 1937. I had gone to the hotel room of the late Bishop Cook of Delaware to talk to him while he packed his bags, for his return to Delaware after the General Convention in Cincinnati.

Bishop Cook told me that Mr. du Pont had resigned from all of his church and school positions because his marriage had ended in divorce. The Bishop told me that he had requested Mr. du Pont "never to embarrass any of the Delaware clergy."

Later I learned that Mr. du Pont, a very sensitive person had interpreted the Bishop's remarks to mean he should never go to the Holy Communion because of his divorce and re-marriage. Actually, Bishop Cook never defined exactly what he had meant.

Mr. du Pont, living then in Rehoboth Beach, Delaware, had been present at my service of consecration in 1939, and had attended the luncheon following, but he had not come forward to meet me. So we had no opportunity to become acquainted, until later.

[92]

In a year or so, he had a serious heart attack and remained in critical condition for a long time. Indeed, his recovery was in question.

Through the grapevine, I received word that Mr. du Pont, confined to his bedroom in Rehoboth Beach, desired the Holy Communion even more than medicine. I must say that, following the conversation with Bishop Cook about not "embarrassing the clergy", Mr. du Pont had continued to go to the Holy Communion service every Sunday, worshipping with the rest of the congregation but declining to go forward to the altar rail to receive the sacrament. He felt this service was absolutely essential, even though he did not himself go forward.

So, following the lead I had received, I found it convenient to ask the able but conservative rector of All Saints' Church, Rehoboth, what his reaction would be if I should request him to administer the Holy Communion to

Mr. du Pont. The rector was very direct and frank. He said he sincerely felt to comply would be contrary to his own convictions.

Since Mr. du Pont was actually a communicant of the Cathedral Church of St. John in Wilmington, I concluded I would follow a somewhat different procedure. I asked the Rehoboth rector to send me a statement, deleting the name of the communicant under discussion but giving all of the pertinent facts about his case. I asked also, that he state his reasons for his inability to give this sick man Holy Communion.

The rector's statement was complete and very well written. I then had copies made and sent to the Reverend Doctor Berton Scott Easton, our great New Testament scholar in those years at General Seminary in New York; to the Reverend Doctor Howard Chandler Robbins, former dean of St. John the Divine in New York, and then a professor at General Seminary; to the Right Reverend Henry St. George Tucker, our Presiding Bishop and a scholar; and to another great New Testament scholar, the Reverend Doctor Frederick Grant of Union Seminary; as well as to several others. I asked each to review the information given about a desperately ill man, to consider all of the facts contained in the statement, and to write me his opinion as to my duty as the Bishop of Delaware.

It was the unanimous, independent opinion of these men that I should show "justice and mercy"—at once. They also stated that their opinion in no way condoned or passed judgment on the divorce and re-marriage. But they felt that by his regular attendance at the early Communion Service in the local parish and by pointedly remaining in his pew at the time the congregation went forward to receive the sacrament, he had not only shown a species of penitence—but also a notable and worthy attitude—an attitude which bespoke of a deep desire for the sacraments of the church.

They also said that they thought it was important to save the life of a man who had been such a devout and helpful churchman throughout his life.

I then wrote to Mr. du Pont's sister, Mrs. Irenee du Pont at Granogue, Delaware, from my summer home in New England, requesting her to call a meeting of her family—her husband and her three then-living brothers. This was promptly arranged. Upon my return, I dined with this group at Granogue.

I told them of the messages I had received, of Mr. du Pont's desire for Holy Communion even more than medicine. I reviewed his record throughout his lifetime as a churchman. I then related how I had asked the rector of the Rehoboth parish to write a scholarly statement concerning all of the facts pertaining to Mr. du Pont's illness and his previous divorce and remarriage, preserving, in the process, Mr. du Pont's anonymity. I told how I had had copies of this statement sent to some of the church's great religious leaders and scholars, asking their independent judgment as to my responsibility as chief pastor of Delaware. I told them how these men had completely agreed it was my duty to show "justice and mercy", and to proceed to try to save a life.

I told the group I wanted to go to Rehoboth with my vestments and private Communion vessels to celebrate the Holy Communion in their brother's sick room. I explained I would rather do this with their knowledge and approval.

The first to speak out cried, "Thank God!" Then, after some discussion, another spoke-up, "Take him our love and best wishes for a speedy recovery."

Armed with family approval and support, I drove to Mr. du Pont's home in Rehoboth. I found him in bed with his Bible on his knee, reading a chapter from St. John's Gospel. He was very friendly, but a little shy, possibly due to his physical weakness. I told him I had just had a meeting with his family and they had sent loving messages to him. There were tears in his eyes. I then told him I had come prepared to hold a Communion service, which outstanding church scholars, including the Presiding Bishop, had unanimously recommended without knowing his identity at all.

Mr. du Pont was quite overcome. He thanked me but said he did not feel strong enough to withstand the emotional strain of the news of my meeting with his family and also the service of Holy Communion, which he had so long desired. He said he would let the dean of the Cathedral in Wilmington know when he felt strong enough to go through the service. He was grateful for my visit. I left him after prayers and a blessing. Later he did partake of the Holy Communion at the hands of the dean of the Cathedral in Wilmington.

I never discussed my procedure with the rector of All Saints' Church because I did not wish to embarrass him. But I must say, with thankfulness, that within a year he came to my office to tell me that he had changed his mind about Mr du Pont and with my approval, he would invite Mr. du Pont and his wife to come regularly to the services of Holy Communion in All Saints' Church. I congratulated him warmly for his understanding and his compassion.

Mr. du Pont gradually improved in health. His wife used to tell me that she strongly felt the reception of the Holy Communion had turned the tide. I emphasized the fact that there was nothing personal in my position, that they were under no obligations whatsoever to the Bishop of Delaware.

With the passing of the years Mr. and Mrs. du Pont became my good friends. When, in 1942, I nearly died of heart exhaustion, due to over-work, Mr. and Mrs. du Pont came to the rescue. First of all, Mr. du Pont persuaded my physician, Dr. William H. Kraemer, who had provided medical care at Bishopstead for many years, to call in the eminent heart specialist, Dr. Wolfert of the

University of Pennsylvania Hospital. Dr. Wolfert took over the case, with Dr. Kraemer acting as his advisor and associate. After a long period of recuperation at Bishopstead, the doctor permitted me to travel, and during the first week in December we entrained for Mr. du Pont's plantation, Combee, situated between Charleston and Savannah.

Mrs. McKinstry and I went there for a prolonged stay so that I might completely recover from my illness. Meanwhile, these good friends provided extra servants to look after our five children at Bishopstead in our absence. This was the only personal thing Mr. and Mrs. du Pont ever did for us, but it was enough to turn the tide to good health, and perhaps save my life.

During the ten years I knew Mr. du Pont I had many talks with him. He had returned to Wilmington to resume his residence here. Our conversations were always about Christian missions, Christian doctrine, church history and similar subjects. Never once did he ever discuss material matters. One would almost have to conclude that he had no interest in money at all. However I have been told that he was one of the few Wilmington men who had anticipated the crash of 1929.

Mr. du Pont was no longer a member of the board of trustees of his beloved St. Andrew's School, although he remained deeply devoted to the school. In June, 1947, I called on him in his Wilmington office to tell him that the school needed to increase the size of his original $1.5 million endowment. Specifically, I pointed out, we needed an additional million dollars to provide necessary scholarships for worthy boys who needed help. Without the slightest hesitation, he promised to deliver the additional million dollars in January of 1948. This he did, very quietly. His original endowment gift, as well as the additional amount in 1948, consisted of Christiana Securities common stock which was then worth perhaps $1,500 per share. In the years that followed these shares became worth about $17,000 each and they split eighty for one. Thus was St. Andrew's School assured of an adequate endowment.

While I was attending the Lambeth Conference of 1948, in London, Mr. du Pont died. His remains were buried at Old St. Anne's Church, Middletown near his St. Andrew's School, and the funeral service was held in the school chapel.

Some years later when his wife, Ann du Pont, decided to move to New York, I asked her if she would please give her spacious home in Rehoboth to the diocese so that we could use it as a conference center. She graciously complied. I also requested an endowment which would be large enough to provide the income required to keep the property in good repair. She said she would. When she died, she left $500,000 for this purpose—much more than I had expected. My successor tried to break the will in this respect, asking the chancellor of Delaware to permit his using the money for other purposes. The request was denied.

Mrs. du Pont's remains were buried beside her husband in Old St. Anne's Cemetery. Her husband had had many years of happy joyous life after his near-disastrous heart attack in 1939. I was grateful to God for his friendship.

It would be quite impossible to mention all of the lay people with whom I had friendly, constructive contacts. However, Mrs. Harry Clark Boden, IV, of Newark, is one whom I would like to mention.

Mrs. Boden's family nickname is "Carita", and that is the name I use whenever we chance to meet. Carita's interests have been quite varied. Years ago she owned a string of racing cars which gained her fame. At one time she had an agency for the Jaguar automobile and, indeed, sought to present the fifth Bishop of Delaware with a Jaguar through the good offices of my son, Jim. Since I had only recently purchased a new Oldsmobile, I had to decline her generous offer. Her interests have been diverse, but I feel sure that her main involvement became the colonial history of our country. She single-handedly restored the Episcopal Church at Earleville, Maryland, and, at about the same time, restored and refurbished Old Shrewsbury Church in the countryside near Kennedyville, Maryland, both in the Diocese of Easton. Later she restored an ancient colonial school house in Elkton, Maryland, and several early colonial churches and other historical buildings in New Jersey and Pennsylvania. All of these restorations she accomplished with her own money, and I have constantly applauded her generosity.

One of her great achievements was the acquisition of the large estate on the Sassafras River, near Cecilton, Maryland, known as "Mt. Harmon". One of Carita's ancestors had owned this plantation in colonial times. However, it passed into other hands, and through the years it had shown the ravages of time and neglect. Carita longed to own "Mt. Harmon", and through intricate diplomacy was able to purchase the remnants of what had once been a grand estate.

No one knows precisely how much the restoration of this estate has cost Carita; but it must have been considerable. The serpentine brick wall has been rebuilt and the wonderful gardens replanted. The mansion now stands proudly, completely restored and furnished with priceless antiques, once again, one of the show places of America, standing as it does among great trees and surrounded on three sides by the waters of the Chesapeake Bay.

Having watched all this—and in a sense having participated in it by lending my encouragement, enthusiasm and praise—I yearned to do something that would produce adequate recognition of Carita's priceless contributions to history. It was my privilege to have the

Mrs. Harry Clark Boden IV

full record of her restorations brought to the attention of Her Majesty, Queen Elizabeth of England.

After a review of all the facts, the Queen decided graciously to honor Carita. A great service was held in the Cathedral of St. John the Divine, New York City. The British ambassador, representing the Queen, made Mrs. Harry Clark Boden, IV a member of the exalted Order of St. John's of Jerusalem, of which the Queen is the titular head. This ancient hospital Order springs from the days of the Crusades. Few Americans have been so honored. Among them are the late Mrs. A. I. du Pont of Nemours, who received a similar honor in 1967 at my suggestion because of her great generosity to the people of England during the Second World War.

Carita continues to do her good works. Recently she deeded "Mt. Harmon" to the National Historical Society, together with a gift of an adequate endowment. I was honored by being permitted to offer the dedicatory prayer on that great occasion.

Throughout my ministry in city parishes the pastoral ministry had been my chief concern. I had served briefly on the staff of St. Paul's Cathedral in Boston; as canon of Grace Cathedral, Topeka; as rector of the Church of the Incarnation, Cleveland; as rector of St. Paul's Church, Albany; as rector of St. Mark's Church, San Antonio, and of Christ Church, Nashville. In all of these posts I had enjoyed a wide pastoral ministry and a wonderful association with competent psychiatrists and medical men.

When I was elected Bishop of Delaware I feared that I would find administrative duties of a Bishop a difficulty which would perhaps block the exercise of a pastoral ministry. However, I was soon permitted to see that I would always have an opportunity to be of help. Especially would this be true in a small, intimate diocese like Delaware. I realized, as I have previously stated, it would take real diplomacy on my part to avoid interfering with the clergy of the several parishes. This I would never do consciously, and I am sure they would never stand for it. I had long before believed the strength of a diocese depends to a great extent on the strength of the pastoral relations between a parish parson and his people.

In due time I began to widen my pastoral contacts with the people. I found it possible and wise to spend a week or ten days in the smaller parishes in lower Delaware. My purpose was to call, with the rector, on all of his people, in their homes. Sometime before I had felt baffled and frustrated because I did not know where the people of a given parish lived or what kind of home life they enjoyed. I also suspected that sometimes the clergy adroitly kept me from knowing their people.

Gradually I was able to convince the rectors it would be great fun for us to call together on the people of the parish. And so, weeks before my arrival in a parish, the rector would arrange a schedule of calls, beginning as early in the morning as possible and always by previous appointment. It was understood that he and I would begin our calling at a decent hour and continue throughout the day until ten o'clock at night. The people of the parish knew when to expect us, and though we never confessed the fact to the people, we planned to stay in each home only twenty or thirty minutes. But this was long enough to make an impact and to accomplish an important pastoral objective.

Many parishioners exclaimed to me, "Never before has a Bishop of the church been in our home."

We always had lunch or dinner in a parishioner's home and we continued to call, as I said, until ten. It took a lot of planning and a lot of energy on the part of the rector to do this work, but it was very worthwhile. This special ministry brought me unspeakable joy.

I may not be too well informed about this, but I have never heard of an Episcopal Bishop in this country who found time to do such extensive house-to-house calling, no matter the size of the diocese.

This plan was an enormous relief to me because I was now able to visit a town and know where the church people lived. I firmly believe this program of calling helped me to build a strong support for any effective diocesan program in the years to come.

Thus assured that my duties as a diocesan administrator would not, after all, cheat me of the privilege of being a pastor, I gradually began to turn to my very important task of forming a forward-looking program. My pastoral contacts had indeed prepared me for a more accurate estimate of the overall needs of a diocesan program. The study preliminary to the launching of the program, as well as the actual compiling of it, proved to be a fascinating enterprise.

Chapter 13

Parishes and Institutions

Upon my arrival in Delaware I became aware of several fine institutions, parishes and missions.

St. Michael's Nursery for Babies on Washington Street had been a credit to the diocese. The nursery had been founded by Bishop Leighton Coleman in a day when there was a great need for an institution to look after infant orphans, or other tots in need.

The foster home-care plan for children had rendered St. Michael's Nursery unnecessary. It was practically empty. So I convinced the board of trustees to close the institution, which had been for white children, and then to sell the property and use the income from the sale and from the endowment (as well as gifts from popular subscriptions) to build St. Michael's Day Nursery for black children on French Street. This was done. However, several attempts were made to force me to close the nursery on French Street. This I refused to do, quite indignantly, as a matter of fact. Today it is one of the finest institutions in the state, and is greatly indebted to Mrs. William C. Lewis, Director, for the remarkable work accomplished under her supervision.

I have already mentioned St. Andrew's School, which was founded, built and endowed by the late Felix du Pont, Sr. It is a great credit to the Diocese of Delaware and to the whole church. The first headmaster was the Rev. Dr. Walden Pell, II. I found him a thoroughly dedicated clergyman, advantaged by schooling at Princeton and Oxford. He was well assisted by his wife, Edith, and a fine faculty.

I gave much time to the school and served as president of the board of trustees throughout my episcopate. Just before I retired, I persuaded the board of trustees to finish the school as it had been originally envisioned by the founder. There was still lacking an adequate library, a good study hall, additional dormitory space and an additional science laboratory, plus the bell tower and auditorium.

The accomplishment came about in a strange way. I had invited two of the trustees of the school to accompany me on a tour of inspection of the campus. We were shocked at the conditions which we found in the "temporary" dormitory over the gymnasium. These quarters were very inadequate.

I asked Dr. Pell how parents of prospective students reacted when shown these quarters. He replied that in many cases the parents left immediately to consider other schools. Following this inspection came the Christmas carol service in the chapel. Since the day happened to mark the twenty-fifth anniversary of Dr. Pell's ordination, he made a speech in which he expressed the wish that he could have been a much better pastor.

Then I responded, disagreeing with his poor assessment of his own service. I described to the students, faculty and the many visitors in the chapel Dr. Pell's embarrassment as he showed us the dormitory quarters over the gymnasium. I apologized to the boys who were required to live in those quarters and announced that the board would proceed at once to finish the school plant as envisioned by the founder. The project would be the twenty-fifth ordination gift to the first headmaster. My announcement—heard by the trustees, faculty, students and guests, including people as prominent as Mrs. Irenee du Pont and members of her family—was a bombshell.

After the carol service, several masters of the school "hooted" me, saying, "Brother, you've got yourself out on a long limb."

St. Andrews School, Middletown, Delaware

Returning home, I engaged a photographer and sent him to the school to photograph the inadequate dormitory over the gymnasium. I sent a print to the trustees, together with a very long letter summoning them to a special meeting of the board to discuss the completion of the school plant. My final statement to them in the letter was that our headmaster had told the trustees during an inspection tour that the school was losing business to competing boarding schools. This unhappy fact was due to conditions for which the trustees were responsible, and I suggested if we had been directors of General Motors and our president were to give a like report, we would either correct the situation or step down.

At the special meeting of the trustees, the late Walter J. Laird, chairman of the trust department of the Wilmington Trust Company and a qualified engineer, protested that it would cost at least a million dollars to build the rest of the plant. (This was, of course, in 1950.) I countered with the statement that no one was equipped to prophesy the exact amount, since as yet we had no plans drawn and no bids.

I convinced the board we should at least authorize the architects to draw plans, to set up specifications and to seek bids.

In due time we were back in session to consider the plans which the board's building committee had approved and to hear the pertinent bids. The total cost came to $800,000. Mr. Laird predicted another $200,000 would be needed to furnish the new buildings and, therefore, his previous estimate was correct. I congratulated him on that fact. Then the question came, "How are you going to finance this? Where is the money coming from?"

I could see the doubt on the faces of the trustees.

"The answer is simple," I said. "We have a sinking fund which now totals over $800,000. Why do we need a sinking fund? Let's cut the balance in the sinking fund in two and add $400,000 to the already-existing

$250,000 in our building fund. This will give us $650,000 to start with.

"Also," I added, "we have, in the offing, a couple of hundred shares of Christiana Securities common stock worth, possibly, $1,500 a share. This stock will come to the trustees in the near future. We will really not need this additional income. Therefore, I suggest we go to the bank and tell them about these shares and borrow the money we need to complete the building. And when the shares come into our hands, we'll sell what is necessary to pay the bills."

I was able to persuade the board this plan was sound, and we soon announced to the public that the building would now be completed as envisioned by the founder.

But the dramatic ending was a surprise, even to me. When Mr. and Mrs. Irenee du Pont saw that the board had sufficient courage and vision to proceed with the completion of the plant, they made a large gift. The sinking fun was never diminished. The Christiana Securities common stock, when it came to us, remained intact. Incidentally, some years later these shares were split eighty for one, giving the school one of the largest endowments of any school of its size in the country.

The completed plant was dedicated by 1957. I was brought out of retirement to assist in the laying of the cornerstone of the new library wing on October 14, 1956.

No boarding school possesses a finer plant. I loved this school and I loved presiding over its board meetings during my episcopate. In recent years, as I have moved about the country attending meetings and dinners, businessman have come up to me saying, "You, sir, confirmed me at St. Andrew's School." Obviously they were proud to make that revelation.

But let us turn to the parishes and missions. What did they look like to the new Bishop in 1939? I was hopeful that the outlying parishes and missions in New

Castle county might in time show signs of growth. While no one could possibly predict the ultimate great influx of people into the county, it did seem fairly reasonable to suppose that the population would increase steadily over the years and that the Episcopal Church was bound to benefit from this fact—an assumption which certainly would prove to be correct.

In the thirty-five years which have elapsed since I became the Bishop of Delaware, tremendous strides have been made under the Bishops of this diocese. Because we all tend to take so many things for granted, it might be helpful to flash back to the beginning of my episcopate to take a look at the diocese for a measure of what progress really has taken place.

The Episcopal clergy of New Castle County in 1939 were deployed as follows: a full-time rector ministered to St. Thomas' Church, Newark, a parish of perhaps 200 communicants, with the additional responsibility for ministering to a small number of Episcopal students at the University of Delaware.

A rector living in the rectory at St. James' Church, Stanton, was also responsible for ministering to the congregation at St. James' Church, Newport, and also to a small congregation at St. Barnabas' Mission, Marshallton. The total communicant strength of all three congregations was not too impressive. At Marshallton, a devoted cathedral layman, Frederick Bringhurst, carried on a valued lay ministry, which was of great assistance to the rector at Stanton and, in fact, to the diocese.

Grace Church, Talleyville, had a loyal congregation but was not very strong in resources. It did have the exclusive services of a rector, however.

Calvary Mission in Hillcrest had originally been founded by the Reverend Charles A. Rantz, rector of the Church of the Ascension, Claymont. However, by the time I became the Bishop this work was now the responsibility of the curate of the Cathedral Church of St. John, the Reverend Joseph C. Wood, who held an evening service in Calvary Mission and, assisted by laymen, tried to promote a small Sunday School. A quaint little stone edifice had been moved from its original location in Carr-croft and served as the mission church. It had a tiny parish house attached.

Our Claymont parish, presided over by the Reverend Mr. Rantz, often boasted that it was somewhat removed from the mainstream of Wilmington church life. It did seem to me to enjoy a species of grand isolation out there in Claymont near the Pennsylvania line.

Immanuel Church, New Castle, was founded in the 17th century. On April 5, 1681, the Reverend John Yeo appeared as the minister—but was soon removed. The Reverend George Keith was then commissioned to make a survey of the opportunity for the colonial church, and he preached in New Castle as early as April 1702. A church was being built in 1703, and was opened for worship in 1706, with the Reverend George Ross as missionary. Immanuel had a most distinguished history and its build- [109] ings, I found, reminded me of quaint English churches. This parish had a full-time resident rector and among the communicants were to be found many loyal and, indeed, distinguished lay people.

The Wilmington city parishes were not unusually robust, it seemed to me. Christ Church, Christiana Hundred, which had long been known as the "Du Pont Church", did not see many large Sunday congregations. I am told an average attendance of thirty-five was about normal, and there were not many more than this attending the Sunday School. I seldom heard about this parish except when time of prominent weddings or funerals were held. The rector, the Reverend Frederick T. Ashton, and his wife, were in my opinion, saints, endowed with patience and deep dedication. However, the congregation was not given to regular attendance, nor did its members have any significant programs in force during the weekdays.

Immanuel Church on Seventeenth Street had a

vigorous rector, the Reverend Doctor Charles W. Clash, who was proud of his people and especially proud of his magnificent church building. He ran the parish single-handed, doing most of the work ordinarily discharged by laymen and vestrymen. He counted the Sunday offerings, he banked the money, he wrote the checks for the treasurer to sign. His parish had fine lay people, but they were not particularly involved in the parish administration.

Trinity Church, at the corner of Delaware Avenue and Adams Street, had a full-time rector, the Reverend Charles F. Penniman, who was an intelligent and competent man. Yet the parish was under-financed and the congregation was far from unified.

St. Andrew's Church, at Eighth and Shipley Streets, had one clergyman, the Reverend R. Ridgely Lytle, Jr., at the time I arrived. The parish was unfortunately torn by tensions, and not in a healthy condition. It had been a happy place under its former rector, the Reverend Doctor Richard W. Trapnell, but at the beginning of my episcopate this parish was extremely shaky.

Old Swedes' Church, under the administrative jurisdiction of Trinity Parish, had a vicar, the Reverend Robert Bell, who was constantly on the alert lest the rector of Trinity overstep his lawful boundary. Old Swedes' had a small, faithful group of people who were extremely proud of the historicity of the church and its beauty. They responded to its needs with the utmost of their capability.

There was also St. Matthew's Episcopal Church on French Street, which ministered to a Negro congregation made up of fine, intelligent people. This congregation occupied two old houses which had somehow been merged into one building—woefully inadequate, most unattractive and desperately in need of better heat and year-round ventilation. The congregation had an independent vicar, the Reverend Adolphus E. Henry, who was devoted to his work and his people.

[110]

Over at Fourth and Rodney Streets was Calvary, the beautiful Bishop Coleman Memorial Church, built by A. Felix du Pont and members of his family, in memory of Mr. du Pont's uncle by marriage, the Right Reverend Leighton Coleman, the second Bishop of Delaware. The church had a faithful priest, the Reverend Doctor George C. Graham, who had always been prominent in diocesan affairs. But there was a distinct shortage of money with which to operate the parish program. I found the church had never been consecrated because of a small remaining debt which I proceeded to liquidate immediately.

The Cathedral Church of St. John, also a beautiful structure, had a dean, the Very Reverend Hiram R. Bennet, and one assistant, the Reverend Joseph C. Wood. The Cathedral buildings had been greatly beautified and enlarged in 1919 by A. Felix du Pont, who was at that time senior warden of the congregation. The congregation, a very loyal group of people, seemed a bit timid about exercising their rights or initiative. No one in the congregation knew for sure the size of the bank balance of the Cathedral because finances were pretty much decided by the senior warden and the bursar, a paid official of the parish. Both were dedicated men who presumably did not wish to bother the members of the congregation with the business details. However, the net result was a lack of lay enthusiasm and little exercise of normal lay stewardship.

There were, therefore, in the greater Wilmington area, including Newark, Claymont and New Castle—approximately thirteen active clergy, some of whom, being charged with several congregations, were spread a bit too thin to be effective. Also, the salaries of the clergy were quite low and indeed money was not very plentiful anywhere—a fact which somewhat surprised me, considering the potential wealth of the area.

At the lower end of the county was the parish of St. Anne's, Middletown, whose historic shrine, Old St. Anne's, Appoquinimink, was surrounded by beautiful burial grounds. The congregation in Middletown was a very hospitable group. But the vestry, as in all cases, was a closed corporation, with the vestrymen re-electing themselves year after year. There was also a small congregation at Delaware City which worshipped in a rather attractive church. Both St. Anne's and Delaware City each had a rector at the time of my coming.

Below Middletown was a church at Smyrna, dignified and stately and with a small, loyal, congregation. The rector was responsible also for the services at a mission church in Clayton, a church which has long since been abandoned. The rectors of Middletown and Smyrna were wonderful men. However, neither was very well-off financially because the standards of giving in both parishes were more of the nineteenth than the twentieth century. The present emphasis on stewardship had not yet become a reality in these congregations.

[112] In Kent County, there was Christ Church, Dover, one of the great historic and distinguished parishes in the diocese. This parish claimed many of the town's most important people. The rector was responsible for services in a nearby church in Camden, Delaware, where a tiny congregation worshipped in a small frame building.

Christ Church, Milford, was the other important historic church in Kent County, although Milford is partially in Sussex County. The rector, the Reverend Joseph S. Hinks, was a faithful and dedicated priest. Prior to his coming to Milford, there had been a long vacancy in the rectorship of the parish and the church had almost been closed. The rector was also in charge of a tiny congregation in Harrington, where he held a Sunday morning service. There were, therefore, two active clergymen in Kent County.

In Sussex County there were only four full-time clergy, deployed as follows: St. Luke's, Seaford, with its responsibility for the church at Bridgeville, where the rector of Seaford conducted Sunday service and whatever weekday services he could find time for. The rector at St. Philip's, Laurel, in addition to his normal parochial duties in that town, had the responsibility for several missions to which he gave as much time as he could. These missions were All Saints' Church, Delmar; St. Mark's Church, Little Creek; St. Andrew's, a country church; and a little church called St. John's. There was also Christ Church outside Laurel, one of the famous early Delaware churches, which held at least one service a year, during the Feast of Pentecost. The rector was in charge of all these congregations and tried to be a pastor to all the people who belonged to them.

At St. Paul's, Georgetown, the rector in residence was also responsible for maintaining the parish of St. Mark's, Millsboro, conducting its services and attending to the pastoral duties there. He was also priest-in-charge of an historic church, Prince George's at Dagsboro, where one or two services were held each year.

The rector of St. Peter's, Lewes, was priest-in-charge of All Saints' Church, Rehoboth Beach, which was then but a summer resort having but few year-round residents. He was also priest-in-charge of the historic St. George's Church, Indian River, with occasional services, especially in the summertime.

St. John's Church, Milton, had no resident clergyman when I came to Delaware but depended on other Sussex clergy for services.

In other words, Sussex County had four active clergymen in charge of all of the parishes and missions of that county. There were, therefore, throughout the entire diocese twenty-two active clergy with more than normal responsibilities.

I think it is fair to say that in no congregation did I detect any great enthusiasm or expectations of great things to come. I rather think that the most enthusiastic parson in the whole diocese was the Reverend Robert Y.

Barber, rector of St. Philip's Church, Laurel. But Brother Barber would have been enthusiastic and full of hope if he had been located in the middle of the Sahara Desert. That was his nature. It was his way of life as long as those around him were orthodox in doctrine and in practice.

I have only the greatest praise for the clergy I found in the diocese in the several parishes and missions. But when vacancies occurred, I felt it incumbent upon me personally to fill these vacancies with strong clergymen. This was a struggle, because money was in short supply for some mysterious reason, in spite of the intrinsic wealth of the diocese.

Chapter 14

Financial Headaches

The program of the diocese in 1939 was, of course, approved by the annual convention of the diocese and then delivered to the executive council for execution. The total diocesan budget for the year was $24,000, of which $15,000 went to the National Council for domestic and foreign missions. The remaining $9,000 had to cover the cost of the executive council's departments, religious education, social service and young people's work. Moreover, it took a major effort to raise the $24,000, despite the fact that Delaware was a state with marvelous resources. The shock of all this nearly floored me.

How could responsible laymen, accustomed to thinking in large terms in business, be content with such an inconsequential sum and such an insignificant program? Nowhere was money readily available for the work of the diocese. For example, my secretary, Miss Elizabeth H. Lightner, who also was the assistant treasurer of the diocese, received the magnificent sum of $100 per month. I immediately gave her my allowance for travel, to help her cope.

I, too was placed in an awkward position by the state of affairs in 1939. When I was elected Bishop I did not inquire into the size of the salary. I thought it of secondary importance. I felt sure that a diocese like Delaware, where there were so many communicants of resources, would see to it that whatever a Bishop needed to pay his bills would be forthcoming.

But I was somewhat mistaken. When I learned that my salary would be $7,000 a year, much less than I had received as a rector, I realized that I was in deep trouble. This sum had to be stretched so as to heat and light drafty old Bishopstead, and to feed, clothe and educate five children and their parents. We had a choice: either we had one or two maids in that enormous house or we would kill Mrs. McKinstry. We also were expected to entertain a considerable number of guests.

I was told upon arrival that I simply must put my three daughters in a private school, although the boys might go to a public school if they wished to. And so, feeling those who informed me were well advised, I enrolled my daughters in Tower Hill School. I think it was rather a wise step, although it did sound a bit snobbish at the time. The boys went to public schools.

It was astonishing to me that there was so little appreciation of the need of special funds, especially for heating and lighting at Bishopstead and for diocesan hospitality. Of course there was nothing I could do about this. I had always held it was unethical for a parson to ask for an increase in salary. Besides, I really believed that God had called me to Delaware and somehow He would solve my dilemma in due time. I regarded the situation merely as another clear-cut indication that the diocese was woefully and inadequately financed. The Bishop's salary came from endowments, and it seemed the people of the diocese had little idea what the salary was. It was never published in any official document, since it was paid by the trustees.

After many months of walking the floor and pondering my unique situation, I decided I would have to go to the bank and borrow some money. So after a year or so, I called on my fellow churchman and wonderful friend, C. Douglass Buck, then the president of the Equitable Trust Company and junior warden of Immanuel Church, New Castle.

When I revealed my mission, he blinked and asked, "How much is your salary, Bishop?"

When I told him he seemed very upset, especially when he learned how far the salary was supposed to stretch. I got the money, but Mr. Buck evidently didn't stop with that, for on his own he quietly contacted trustees of the diocese, and other prominent fellow churchmen. Before long, the trustees informed me that a sum of $3,000 per year would be forthcoming for the heating and lighting of Bishopstead and for other extras. Sometime later, the convention of the diocese raised my salary to a more adequate amount.

I was glad this came about without any plea from me. I really look back upon the situation with a bit more than ordinary interest because I believe the step the trustees took—under pressure I must admit—was the beginning of a quickened sense of their responsibility in diocesan affairs.

The trustees of the diocese, a body which approximated a Bishop's vestry made up of top laymen, served for a term of three years and were eligible to succeed themselves if re-elected by the convention. The trustees controlled the endowments left to the diocese. The income was allocated by them, and many parishes and missions placed their endowments and capital funds in their hands. The trustees were advised by an eminent banking firm—Brown Brothers Harriman of New York.

I thought this was a top group of people, able and consecrated, and the diocese owed them all a great debt of gratitude. They were not money-raisers. They faithfully dispensed the moneys placed in their hands. During my episcopate I valued my contacts with this body of men, as I did with the executive council members who also were faithful in the discharge of their duties.

I think, however, that in almost every instance, whether it was the executive council or the trustees or the standing committee (which is the official legal body of the diocese, next to the Bishop) there was a need for opening new vistas, new understandings of what the church might accomplish in the State of Delaware.

It seemed evident that if we were to have a greater feeling of stewardship on the part of the people in the congregations and in the diocese at large, we had to have better leadership in the respective parishes and missions. We had to have men who would "inform the minds and awaken the consciences" of the people before the financial situation could be greatly remedied.

But before proceeding with this objective, I felt it necessary to arouse young laymen and bring them to an annual lay conference, which I caused to be held each September with the help of the headmaster, Dr. Walden Pell, at St. Andrew's School. Charles W. Wendt, a member of St. Andrew's Parish, took the lead in this matter. He was accustomed to creating and executing programs, and he had a gift for promotion. He was ably assisted by W. Albert Haddock and Manfred Keller and Harry G. Haskell, Jr., all from Trinity Parish in Wilmington. Governor Elbert N. Carvel of Laurel also was a great help in these conferences, as was Houston Wilson, a lawyer from Georgetown.

There was a very good representation from all of the parishes and missions of the diocese at these conferences. Distinguished church leaders, like the Presiding Bishop, the Right Reverend Henry St. George Tucker, came to lead the conferences and to address the men on the programs of the church outside the diocese. I am proud to report the conferences seemed to light new fires of enthusiasm in the parishes and it was the beginning of a new life throughout the diocese.

But the thought which haunted me constantly, as I moved about in an attempt to arouse the people, was that the diocese greatly needed a thorough survey of the parishes and missions which could be used as a basis for projecting a ten-year program, giving the diocese a track to run on. How could we approach this subject without seeming to be critical of the diocese and of those who had led the church in the past?

I recognized from the very beginning that Delawareans were very sensitive, proud people. I did not wish to provoke them or to appear to them as being too aggressive.

However, before proceeding with my attempt to get the diocese committed to an intensive survey, I returned again and again to my conviction that what the diocese needed, was a strong body of clergy. And every time we had the opportunity we sought to bring an understanding clergyman to the diocese. For example, the Reverend Arthur Lichtenberger, then rector of St. Paul's Church, Brookline, Massachusetts, and later, I say with pride, the Presiding Bishop of the Episcopal Church, was called to St. Andrew's Church in Wilmington. Despite the fact that he and I had been college fraternity mates and friends for many years, I was unable to get him to accept the call to Delaware. I am sure that the salary was not attractive to him.

Again, the Reverend Stephen Bayne, who in later years became one of the great Bishops of the Anglican Communion, and who at that time was chaplain at Columbia University, was asked by me to come to Wilmington and to consider a call to Trinity Church. He declined. Finances obviously had something to do with it.

The effect of limited resources and small salaries on the calling of a rector can be illustrated by what happened at Christ Church, Dover, following the resignation of the saintly canon, Benjamin F. Thompson, who had served in that parish for twenty or twenty-five years.

I was invited to lunch with the vestry of Christ Church, at the historic and beautiful home of the late Henry Ridgely, who was president of the Farmers' Bank of Delaware and senior warden of the parish. The men of the vestry were bankers, businessmen, lawyers, judges and one was state superintendent of schools. After a delightful luncheon Mrs. Ridgely had prepared I asked the men to describe the kind of a rector they felt the parish needed at that time. Although they had not called a man for nearly a quarter of a century, the men quite glibly listed the necessary qualifications as they saw the situation, and it was evident that they had been giving some careful thought to the matter. They said the new rector must be a parson with a fine family background. He must have an excellent education. He must be a wonderful administrator and an outstanding pastor, faithfully willing to call on his flock. He should be an expert in the field of religious education, a man who knew how to develop young people's work. He should be a community-minded man who would cooperate with the other churches in Dover.

They went on and on, and finally they wound up their superman list of qualifications by adding, "Of course, we would be delighted if you could find us a man who was also a competent musician, perhaps an organist."

Naturally I gasped. Then, putting on my best poker face I said to them, "Gentlemen, how much do you intend to pay such a paragon?"

I looked at Mr. Ridgely, who couldn't see me because he was blind, but with a thoughtful expression on his countenance he replied, "The salary will be $1,800 a year. And, of course the use of the rectory."

I tried to be as courteous as I could. I said to them, "In other words, gentlemen, you want a new rector who will match any man in this room in background, in education and ability."

They agreed that that was what they wanted. Then I asked quickly "Gentlemen, is there an $1,800 a year man in the room?"

Silence. Then a broad grin came on the face of

the senior warden. He said, "We get you. How much should we pay?"

I named a figure, adding that this was predicated on our finding a young clergyman with all the qualifications. The amount I had stated was considerably more than they had envisioned, of course, but they showed no signs of arguing and seemed only a little shocked. Then they authorized me to find a man who would meet the specifications and they would gratefully pay what was necessary, although it would be difficult at first to raise all the money required. Looking around the table, I doubted that this would prove to be true.

I really performed a miracle. Through dear friends in Albany, I learned of the Reverend Paul A. Kellogg, who was married to a priceless wife, Helen, and who lived in Ticonderoga, New York, where he was rector of the Church of the Cross. He was the son of a scholar and the grandson of a great missionary to India who, I think, had translated the Bible into Hindi. He was a Princeton man and he was also educated at General Seminary and Union Seminary in New York.

[121]

I called on Mr. Kellog in Ticonderoga and was most impressed. I felt he met the specifications in every way. He was called and I am glad to say he accepted.

The Kellogs lived in Christ Church rectory for at least sixteen years. It was a truly wonderful experience for Christ Church and the diocese. The Kelloggs participated in every aspect of the church's work in the diocese. Mr. Kellogg was on every board and committee, I think. Mrs. Kellogg was the leader in the women's auxiliary of the diocese. Eventually, the House of Bishops elected Paul Kellogg to be missionary Bishop to the Dominican Republic, where he served with extreme distinction. Bishop and Mrs. Kellogg, having concluded their mission to the Dominican Republic, have returned to Delaware and are in residence in Dover. At the time of this writing (1974), he was serving as assistant to the Bishop of Pennsylvania.

Another example of an effort to fill a vacancy involves St. Anne's Church in Middletown. The rector of this parish, the Reverend Percy L. Donaghay, had been in the post for a great number of years. It was necessary for him to retire and a successor had to be found. I met with the vestry, which had not had much experience in finding rectors. They turned to me for help.

In a conference with the vestry, the senior warden, Dr. James Gaylord Bragden, a pharmacist, told me he had listened frequently to the broadcast of religious services from Holy Trinity Church, Rittenhouse Square, Philadelphia, and that he had noted the wife of the assistant there had been substituting at the organ on Sunday morning. He was very much impressed with her playing and he said to me, "You know, sir, we need an organist even more than we need a rector."

[122]

The vestry discussed all of this with me, stressing the fact that they liked the preaching of the assistant at Trinity who was in charge of the services during the summer. They, too, emphasized the wife's musical skill. So they asked me if I could try to persuade the rector of Holy Trinity Church to permit Mr. Smith and his wife to conduct a service on Sunday morning. This is a procedure which I always frowned on, but in this case, since the assistant at Holy Trinity was willing to come, I let it go at that.

I invited the assistant and his wife to spend Saturday night at old Bishopshead. They were very pleasant people whom I had once known in Texas. The next morning I drew a road map showing them how to reach Middletown by car. I explained the service was at eleven o'clock, but the vestry wanted them there at ten so they could have a conference before the service. Saying good-bye, the couple from Rittenhouse Square drove off.

I heard nothing more until late that night after I had returned from a heavy schedule downstate and was resting in my study. It seems the assistant and his wife drove through Middletown without realizing it.

They stopped their car a little beyond Middletown and asked a farmer if he could direct them to St. Anne's Church. The farmer, not a member of the Episcopal Church but interested in historic things, explained, "Oh, yes, wonderful Old St. Anne's. You go down this country road south and after two miles you turn to the left and you will come to dear Old St. Anne's, Appoquinimink. You will love it."

It was late in the fall and it was sprinkling. The couple followed the farmer's instructions and found themselves at historic St. Anne's which, of course, was shuttered and locked because it wasn't due to open until the following June. The young couple sat on the moist tombstones in the churchyard, waiting expectantly for the vestry to show up and for the sexton to come and open the church. They waited and they waited—but nothing happened.

Meanwhile, in town at the year-round parish church of St. Anne's, the vestry was out front, looking anxiously for the young clergyman and his wife. The congregation had been routed out of their homes by promises of a fine service and a great sermon, as well as a look at a most charming prospective organist. Many visitors were present. The church was packed by eleven o'clock. The choir, usually somewhat smallish, had been augmented by what might be called "ringers". Everything was ready. But where was the clergyman?

A young man who had just been elected treasurer of the church looked over the Easter-size congregation with great glee. It would be a fine way to start off his career as a treasurer.

By 11:15 a.m., Dr. Bragden proceeded down the aisle to face a puzzled and somewhat anxious congregation. He said, "We do not know where the young man from Rittenhouse Square is. He and his wife may have met with foul play. They may be lying wounded and bleeding somewhere along the roadside. We sincerely trust his dear wife has not been injured. But in any event he is not here and so we cannot hold you longer in good conscience."

The congregation was dismissed, and while the vestrymen stood out in front talking about this terrible turn of events, a young man and his wife, driving a car with a Pennsylvania license, dashed up the church at twelve-thirty. Very perturbed and embarrassed, the Pennsylvanians blurted out, "Why didn't someone tell us there were two St. Anne's churches?"

A vestryman spoke quickly in an aside to Dr. Bragden: "Now, Doc, take another look at this charming lady. You know we need an organist very much. Don't be too hasty. Invite them over to your house."

So the confused and upset couple accompanied by the vestrymen, went to the home of Dr. Bragden, where they had a wonderful time and everything was forgiven. They hoped very much that the assistant, even though he hadn't preached, would consider a call to St. Anne's, Middletown.

Shortly after one o'clock, Dr. Bragden explained to his guests that they were to have lunch at St. Andrew's School and he carefully explained to them how to get there. He told them that Doctor Pell was a distinguished clergyman who had been a Rhodes scholar, and had rowed on the crew of Christ Church, Oxford. He also said wonderful things about the school. He gave an affectionate good-bye to the guests and sent them off to St. Andrew's School and to lunch, having explained where Doctor Pell's residence was on the campus.

When they got to Doctor Pell's home they rang the bell long and loud but, of course, by this time it was one-fifteen, and Doctor Pell, the faculty of the school and their leaders, plus all of the students, were waiting for their guests in the great dining hall of St. Andrew's School.

There was no note on the door explaining things, and so by this time completely upset and befuddled, the Philadelphians got back into their car and found their way back to Rittenhouse Square, where it is said, they went into Holy Trinity Church, got down on their knees and said in fervent prayer, "O Lord, if you'd just let us remain safely in Rittenhouse Square, never again will we wander forth into the wilds of Delaware."

Chapter 15

More About Rectors

Since those early days in my episcopate, I learned a lot more about wonderful Delaware, and it was possible to attract able clergy to the diocese.

The vestry at St. Anne's, Middletown, was able to persuade the Reverend Kenneth E. Clarke, an assistant at the Cathedral in Wilmington, to be their rector. He brought his wife, Amelia, daughter of the Reverend and Mrs. Frederick T. Ashton.

During Mr. Clarke's leadership, the beautiful new parish house was built. The parish resources, both spiritual and material, noticeably improved, and in due time Mr. Clarke was called to an unusual parish near Cincinnati. He has been in Ohio ever since and is now in charge of a retirement home operated by the Diocese of Southern Ohio.

In Wilmington, the Reverend John Ellis Large, formerly chaplain of St. Andrew's School and an excellent English master, had come to St. Andrew's Church in Wilmington. Not only did he save that parish, he stimulated it into greater power and influence than it had ever experienced in all of its long history. After ten years there, he was called to the Church of the Heavenly Rest, Fifth Avenue, New York, to be its rector.

In 1943, Calvary Church at Fourth and Rodney Streets called the Reverend Henry N. Herndon, who had been rector at Plattsburg in the Diocese of Ohio. I had first known Henry Herndon in West Texas, where he had been rector of the church in Uvalde, the home of Vice President John Nance Garner. I was enthusiastic about the Herndons coming to Calvary Church, since he was among the most dedicated, devout priests I have ever known. He had a great concern for the welfare of people, which was evidenced by the fact that, in addition to his parish duties, he served as chaplain at the Delaware State Hospital for many years. No clergyman ever gave so much of his time and love and strength in the interest of human rights and the welfare of ordinary people.

In 1946, the Reverend Donald J. Parsons became rector of our church in Smyrna. After an effective ministry there, he was called to be a professor at our theological seminary, Nashota House, in Wisconsin. He now is the Bishop of Quincy (Illinois).

In 1948, I persuaded the Reverend Theodore L. Ludlow to come from the Oranges in New Jersey to be rector of St. Thomas' Church, Newark. Under his long rectorship, a beautiful new church was erected. He has been one of the most faithful clergy in the Diocese of Delaware.

I slipped over the boundary of our diocese into the Diocese of Easton (Maryland), to spy on a young parson who was, at the time, temporarily in charge of the church at Church Hill, Maryland.

This young man, the Reverend James O. Reynolds, with a family background in New Orleans and South Carolina, had been recommended to me as a possible chaplain for St. Andrew's School, Middletown. I liked him, and he was shortly afterwards called to that post, where he served with notable distinction. The boys called him "Straight Arrow".

Later, Jim Reynolds became the rector of Immanuel Church, New Castle. He subsequently surprised his congregation by accepting a challenging work at St. Augustine's, Bohemia Manor, near Chesapeake City,

Maryland. His has been an outstanding ministry and he has been president of the standing committee of the Diocese of Easton.

In 1951, we were able to persuade the Reverend Richard S. Bailey to come from Ocean City, New Jersey, to All Saints' Church, Rehoboth Beach. I need not dwell on the effectiveness of his long rectorship. He and his wife, Charlotte, have been beloved of the people.

The Reverend Charles M. Priebe, Jr., became the rector of St. James' Church, Newport, in 1952, and continued an effective ministry there throughout the years.

The Reverend Victor Kusik, following his ordination, was sent by me to St. Mary's Mission in Bridgeville, in 1952. He gave the people a wonderful ministry for some eighteen or more years. Since then he has become the rector of the important Immanuel Church, Wilmington.

Also in 1952, the Reverend Frank L. Moon was brought by me from Maryland to St. Peter's, Lewes. Here again we had a strong pastoral ministry throughout the years because of the dedication of this man and his dear wife, Barbara.

That same year, we called the Reverend F. Sydney Bancroft, Jr., from the Diocese of New Jersey to the church in Smyrna. He was able to perform miracles there and was then called to be canon at the Cathedral Church of St. John, Wilmington, where he has served for many years and is most beloved. He and Mrs. Bancroft (Sylvia) are exceptional people.

The Reverend John Wilson Haynes was called from Rhode Island to be rector of Calvary Church, Hillcrest, in 1953. He had a long and profitable ministry there, and under his leadership the parish grew in every aspect.

In 1954, I went to Crozier Seminary in Chester and tapped Marvin Heber Hummel and helped him realize his desire to leave another denomination for membership in the Episcopal Church. He was in due time ordained and served effectively as a chaplain to students at the University of Delaware.

When the Reverend Charles F. Penniman resigned from Trinity Church, Wilmington, to undertake a diocesan task in St. Louis, the vacancy was filled by the Reverend Donald W. Mayberry, who had just returned from serving as a Navy chaplain in the Pacific during the Second World War. After a fine rectorship at Trinity, Mr. Mayberry was called to the rectorship of historic St. John's in Lafayette Square, Washington, D.C., known as the church of the presidents.

When the Very Reverend Hiram R. Bennett resigned from the Cathedral Church of St. John, we nominated the Reverend Robert M. Hatch to come from Arlington, Massachusetts, to be the new dean. Within a very few years he was called to be rector of St. John's Church, Waterbury, Connecticut, one of the leading parishes in New England. From that post he was shortly elected to be Suffragan Bishop of Connecticut, and later he became the Bishop of Western Massachusetts, and only recently retired from the active ministry.

[129]

After Doctor Large resigned from St. Andrew's, Wilmington, we were able to persuade the Reverend William H. Marmion to become the rector of that church. Mr. Marmion had been my associate for a number of years at St. Mark's Church in San Antonio, and later he was rector of St. Mary's Parish Church, Birmingham, Alabama. Following an effective ministry here, he became the Bishop of Southwestern Virginia, where he is still active and doing a great work.

Mr. Marmion was succeeded by the Reverend Richard M. Trelease. He had been dean of St. Andrew's Cathedral, Honolulu. I had been after Dean Trelease for some time. Indeed, I made a special trip to Honolulu with my wife to investigate his work there. Mr. Trelease had a wonderful ministry at St. Andrew's and from there he was called to the important parish of St. Paul's, Akron. Recently he became the Bishop of New Mexico, now called the Diocese of the Rio Grande.

Following Mr. Trelease's resignation, the Reverend Gordon T. Charlton became rector of St. Andrew's Church. He was a man of deep religious conviction and an able teacher and preacher. He had been a boy in my parish at San Antonio when I was the rector there. At the end of a fruitful ministry, he became a member of the faculty of the Virginia Seminary and has now become the dean of the Episcopal Seminary in Austin, Texas, and is regarded as one of our most interesting administrators and scholars.

While I was attending the Lambeth Conference in London in 1948, I received word from the Cathedral vestry in Wilmington that it would like permission to call [130] the Reverend J. Brooke Mosley, who was on the staff of the Bishop of Washington at that time. I had not known Mr. Mosley, so I conferred with the Bishop of Washington, Bishop Dun, and also Bishop Henry Wise Hobson of Southern Ohio about him. Both men were very enthusiastic about Mr. Mosley. He had worked under them both. And so, after a careful investigation, I cabled the standing committee of Delaware and the vestry of the Cathedral that I would give my permission, adding that I was sorry I could not be on hand to help them in the process. He was called to be dean of the Cathedral Church of St. John, and he accepted.

Upon my return from London I went to Washington to meet the Mosleys. I found Betty Mosley a beautiful and most charming person. Mr. Mosley had had a fine career before coming to Wilmington and surely he was one of the best deans we could have had. He did many things that were needed, he brought about many improvements to the plant. He was an excellent pastor, a good preacher and very much admired.

So, little by little, Delaware grew in its attractiveness, and I was able to bring to the diocese strong clergymen much needed to arouse the consciences of the people and increase their sense of stewardship.

Chapter 16

The Diocese Is Surveyed

While reading the previous diocesan journals, I chanced to note Bishop Philip Cook's message to the last convention over which he presided before his death in 1937. In that address he had asked the convention to authorize a thorough survey of the diocese for the purpose of building a forward-looking program. The convention had voted unanimously for it and had committed the matter into the hands of the executive council. I nearly jumped for joy.

At the next meeting of the executive council I put on my best poker face and asked the council to let me see a copy of the survey. The members looked at one another blankly.

"What survey?"

I said, "The survey which was the last request of your beloved Bishop. Let me read you the action of the convention."

They were embarrassed, and told me they didn't have the survey, that it had never been conducted and they didn't know how to do it.

"But," I said, "this was, after all, the last request of your Bishop. Don't you intend to carry out his last request?"

They took the hint and voted that, if I would show them how to do it, they would authorize and conduct a survey. I said I would help.

I had been Bishop of Delaware long enough to realize that a survey was very much needed before we

Bishop Philip Cook, Fourth Bishop of Delaware

could plan for the years ahead. When I was able to reach an agreement with the executive council of the diocese and proceed with its full and enthusiastic support, I communicated with the Reverend Doctor David Covell, secretary of the Forward Movement Commission, headquartered in Cincinnati. He was an expert in such matters, and I asked him to come to Delaware, to meet with me and several members of the diocese in a discussion of the survey.

Dr. Covell came with great enthusiasm, and discussed the whole subject with firm knowledge and understanding of all the implications. He tactfully requested that each congregation survey itself according to well-established guidelines. In this way we would avoid the suspicion that we were going into a parish or mission and embarrass its members—or make them do things they didn't wish to do. We wanted to avoid giving the impression that we were trying to impose something on the people. And so each congregation would have its own survey, conducted by the vestry under the guidance of the rector and participated in by people representing all phases of parish life. The survey posed the questions, but the people supplied their own answers.

Doctor Covell agreed to see that the survey was properly conducted. I, therefore, appointed a diocesan-wide survey committee and put top people on it. When at last the survey was concluded, after many months of work, and we were having our first report meeting, Doctor Covell read his findings and his recommendations. Some of the latter seemed to be a slight rebuke to certain parishes but tactfully delivered. The proposed program, based upon information the parishes had themselves supplied, was far-reaching—but always within reason, and within the resources of the parishes and missions and the diocese at large.

Doctor Covell, for example, reported on Christ Church Christiana Hundred in these words: "I have made several attempts to get into this church between Sundays, but each time I have found the doors of the church and the parish house locked."

He added that he had come to the rueful conclusion that very little, if anything, ever happened in Christ Church parish except on Sunday mornings. He reported that the Sunday morning attendance was apparently about thirty-five and that there were about the same number in Sunday School. The three prominent members of Christ Church vestry who served on this diocesan survey committee listened very soberly but made no comment.

Six months later, the senior warden of Christ Church, Henry Francis du Pont, asked me to a men-only dinner at Winterthur his home. When I arrived I found that the group included the entire vestry of Christ Church, but not the rector, Reverend Frederick T. Ashton. This bothered me—was he being ignored? I loved the rector. After a delicious dinner, the host took us into the library. He apologized to me for the absence of the rector. He explained this was not intended as a slight because he and the vestry had deep affection for the rector. [135]

"We have to talk to you about the diocesan survey report by Doctor Covell," he said. "We admit that Doctor Covell told the truth about us, and we are most unhappy about our situation. We can see other parishes of the diocese moving ahead. We want to do better, but how can we go about it?"

I asked, "How many vestry meetings do you hold each year?" They told me quite sincerely that ordinarily they had one vestry meeting a year—a meeting to re-elect themselves as vestrymen and to hear the treasurer's reports. Seeing my shocked look, they asked, "Well, how many should we have? No one has ever told us."

I explained the usual procedure was to hold at least ten, and I also pointed out that the wardens and the vestrymen of the parish had a special responsibility for the program of the parish, that it was not the rector's job alone.

The group assured me that they would do anything required to get the parish moving. So I suggested that they engage an assistant clergyman to help with the parish calling, and the running of the Church School. I also proposed that they recruit and pay Sunday school teachers from West Chester Teachers' College (as it was then known) or the University of Pennsylvania— fine young church men and women—who would be capable of serving as top flight teachers in their Church School on Sundays.

The vestry was intrigued with both suggestions and ratified them at once. I then suggested that the senior warden appoint a committee of two vestrymen to call on the rector and to offer these assistances to him. I asked the vestry never to reveal that it had held the meeting without the rector, that this would certainly break his heart. I cautioned the committee to avoid embarrassing or hurting him.

In a few days, the Reverend Mr. Ashton came to my office in a great state of excitement, bubbling with news of the wonderful proposals made to him by his vestry. I urged him to proceed at once to find an assistant and gave him several other suggestions. I also urged him to undertake the engagement of top-flight Church School teachers as well, pointing out that his Sunday School would then become the first one in the state and one of the few in the East, with top-flight, paid Sunday School teachers. The rector left, very happy and talking of "the dawning of a new day at Christ Church".

Six months went by, and one day a member of the special committee, which had called on the rector, asked me to have lunch with him and another member of the vestry. They reported that no progress had been made. Nothing had been done to find an assistant or to look into the possibility of engaging teachers for the Sunday School. The committee reported to me the vestry now felt it must frankly discuss the situation with the rector, possibly suggesting that he find another parish.

I was very upset about this development. I cautioned the men against breaking a fine man's heart. I said, "After all, he's been the kind of a rector you wanted all these years. He's a godly man. You can't expect him suddenly to pick up and become young again in his outlook, and in step with present-day policies of modern parishes."

I knew they were going to meet the rector that night at vestry meeting and I waited patiently, hoping the rector would come to see me about the meeting. But he did not come. I was so troubled about the effect on the rector's morale, I really couldn't sleep at night.

So, unwilling to wait any longer, I cooked up an excuse to drive to St. Michael's on the Eastern Shore of Maryland and to call on someone there about an insignificant piece of business. I asked Mr. Ashton to go with me for company.

Nothing was said during our ride to St. Michael's about Christ Church, or the meeting of the vestry. But on our way back, the rector asked me how well I knew Bishop William T. Manning. I said I knew the Bishop quite well. He said, "Would you be willing to suggest to Bishop Manning that he appoint me as a hospital chaplain in New York?" He added that he had always wanted to be a hospital chaplain.

Then the rector discussed Christ Church and the need of a more modern parish program which he felt unable to launch. He had ten more years to go before retirement and I thought he had much to give. So I explained to him the Diocese of Delaware really needed a hospital chaplain very much. The hospitals were beginning to boom in Wilmington, and increasing numbers of patients were coming from all over the state and beyond. I told him

I would be happy to propose to the diocesan convention, that a hospital chaplain be appointed in Wilmington, and, if this happened, I would then proceed to appoint him to the post. He said he was very happy about this prospect.

The next day, I reported this to the special committee of the vestry of Christ Church, pointing out that the vestry would have to be responsible for providing the chaplain's salary for ten years, as well as supplying him with a house and an automobile. Although there were no diocesan funds available for such a purpose, the vestry enthusiastically and generously agreed to do all of this.

Therefore, I went before the next meeting of the diocesan convention to request the authorization of the position of hospital chaplain in Wilmington, with the understanding that the diocese would not be financially responsible in any way. This was voted unanimously, and it was left up to the Bishop to appoint the chaplain.

[138] Of course, I appointed the rector of Christ Church, and he served as hospital chaplain for ten years, and most effectively. The Reverend Mr. Ashton was a man of priceless humor and not given to long conversations, which made him an excellent visitor to the sick.

In due time, I nominated the Reverend Doctor William Capers Munds, then rector of the Church of the Good Shepherd, Corpus Christi, Texas, as successor to the resigned rector of Christ Church. I had known Doctor Munds for a long time. Indeed, it was I who nominated him to his position in Corpus Christi. On that occasion, I went to Cleveland to present the call to him. He was then rector of the Church of the Incarnation—a church which I had built some years before.

I was very happy when Doctor Munds decided to come to Delaware to study the situation. We were proposing that he leave a great parish in Corpus Christi—a parish which he had built-up during eight years of fruitful ministry—to accept the call to a small parish outside Wilmington. However, he saw the great challenge at

Christ Church, and so he accepted the call and was in residence late in October, 1942.

With his knowledge, experience and abilities, things began to move in Christ Church. By 1960 the parish had increased in size from 150 communicants to over 1,000, the Church School from 35 to at least 500. When Doctor Munds retired in 1960, the Reverend Dr. John L. O'Hear, an able clergyman and former rector of St. Paul's, Cleveland Heights, succeeded him. Doctor O'Hear has carried Christ Church to great heights. Today the church is a vital factor in the life of the community and the state.

The budget of this parish has continued to grow, by leaps and bounds. The Christ Church congregation is one of the greatest supporters of missions and theological education of any parish in the country. Thus the survey which was begun by Doctor Covell, in this single instance, more than justified all the effort which was expended in making it a reality. [139]

The Covell survey had also called attention to the population expansion in Hillcrest, outside Wilmington. After much thought, it seemed advisable to me to place a full-time clergyman at Calvary Mission. The Reverend Robert Gilson was moved to Hillcrest from St. Luke's Church in Seaford to be Calvary's first full-time vicar. This mission became a great success through the years; growth was quite evident immediately. The mission became an independent parish in a very short time. Within a few years a new church plant was a necessity.

But where would I get the money to build one? I knew the congregation would not contribute very much to a new church project. When I broke ground for the new Calvary Church (to be the Bishop Cook Memorial Church) I had actually no money. Seeing my faith and determination, one rich layman sent me a check for $35,000 and another great churchwoman sent a check for $50,000.

The rest was easy. Both gifts were entirely unsolicited on my part.

It seems unnecessary to list all of the instances of growth which followed the challenge of the Covell survey. St. James', Stanton, improved its plant. New rectories were built in Newark and at Christ Church Christiana Hundred. A beautiful church was built in Newport and in later years a new church in St. Thomas' parish, Newark.

In Sussex County, a summer church was built at Bethany Beach; in Georgetown, a parish house was built while the Reverend Richard K. White was the rector; at St. Peter's Church in Lewes there was a new parish house built—also new parish houses for All Saints', Rehoboth Beach, and at St. John's, Milton. A new church and parish house were built in Selbyville.

In Kent County, Christ Church, Dover, built a fine new parish house. In Middletown, an adequate parish house was built and also an addition was made to the parish house in Talleyville. Improvements were made to the church plants at St. Andrew's, Wilmington, and at Immanuel Church on Seventeenth Street in Wilmington.

One of the achievements I was most proud of was the new parish church built for St. Matthew's in Wilmington. For a long time I had been quite disgusted with the miserable quarters occupied by this congregation. I began to talk about the necessity of a decent church there on French Street. With the help of a fine friend, Frederick Bringhurst (that great layman who knew where there was some good Quaker money) I determined that a new church would indeed be built at Seventh and Walnut Streets. It was a great venture of faith. I hope it has proved justified in the years later. Joseph Holton Jones was the architect, and for him it was indeed a labor of love.

St. David's Church on Grubb Road was another project which came along. Through the great generosity of a Presbyterian layman the land was given to the diocese for the new church. When the first unit was completed, I assigned the Reverend J. Seymour Flinn to be the vicar of this congregation and he did a very fine piece of work laying the foundation for future years.

The architect for the new buildings, except St. Matthew's, was William H. Thompson of Philadelphia. He was the son of the late Canon Benjamin F. Thompson, who had served as rector of Christ Church, Dover, for twenty or more years. He was very much beloved throughout the diocese. This fine architect also designed and supervised the construction of the parish house at Christ Church, Wilmington, built under Doctor Munds' leadership. He designed and supervised the construction of the new wing at St. Andrew's School, Middletown. He must have presided over $4,000,000 worth of construction during my episcopate.

Our builder was W. Albert Haddock, one of the able churchmen of the diocese and a distinguished contractor. We owe much to him. Every aspect and detail of our expanding diocesan program had, of course, the hearty endorsement and assistance of our executive council.

Chapter 17

The Diocese Leads the Way

Our diocesan survey had predicted great growth in areas near Stanton, Marshallton and Newport, where only one clergyman had been needed through the years to take care of three tiny congregations. The survey suggested that there would be a population explosion in Brandywine Hundred which would require more churches. Before long, we began to look south of Wilmington to a place called Wilmington Manor where there was as yet no church of any denomination. I requested Harry G. Haskell, Jr., who owned the Greenhill Dairies and who was serving at the time as chairman of the strategy committee of the diocese, to have his delivery men carry on a careful investigation of the area and tell me how many children lived there.

Soon we decided to purchase a large stone barn in that growing area and this became the Church of the Nativity. Here we enlisted the skill of Joseph Holton Jones to convert the barn into a lovely church.

It goes without saying that many of the items proposed in the survey would depend upon adequate funding. Always we have been short of cash when we proposed anything of a diocesan nature. Therefore, I conceived the idea of what I called an "advance fund". I envisioned a large fund which could be utilized by the parishes when they felt the necessity of building to meet their needs and opportunities. We were the first diocese in the nation to think up such a scheme as this. Later-on almost every diocese adopted the plan.

How could the people of the diocese be

Harry G. Haskell, Jr., Esq.

Joseph W. Chinn, Esq.

persuaded to back such an idea? One of the first things I did was to call on businessmen to learn if they thought it would be a feasible plan. I remember calling on the late Pierre S. du Pont and discussing the matter with him in detail. He not only approved of the idea but he said he would be glad to give to the fund.

I then convinced the executive council and the convention of the diocese to take this step, modestly suggesting an objective of $250,000. I appointed Captain Hudson D. Dravo, United States Navy, to assist me in putting over this fund.

After the initial publicity, and after the brochures had been printed and distributed, I met Harry Haskell in the old Wilmington Country Club and listened to what he had to say.

He said, "Bishop, you are too timid about this fund. Delaware is going to boom, and I think you should go after a million dollars rather than a paltry $250,000."

I told him I was finding it very difficult to raise the smaller sum because the whole concept—lending construction money to parishes for fifteen years at one per cent interest annually—was altogether new.

I knew that Mr. Haskell was right, but I was so anxious to raise the smaller amount and so afraid that I couldn't, I was content to stay with the smaller goal.

Much to my surprise, within a day after my discussion of the matter with Mr. Haskell he sent me a very large check toward the fund—the largest single contribution made by anyone. We met our goal.

Doctor Covell's survey had also called attention to the need of a more adequate program for the young people of the diocese. This, too, would cost a lot of money. The diocese had never had a conference camp center or a program for young people of any great size, although Bishop Cook had maintained a small camp on Silver Lake near St. Andrew's School for boys.

I had had a lot of experience with church camps

and conferences for young people, having originated a camping program in the Diocese of West Texas while I was rector at St. Mark's Church, in San Antonio. That diocese has made a great success of its young people's program, its camps and conferences, and now conducts three large camp-conference centers, to which several thousand youngsters go each summer. And each summer, after the youngsters are through with their camping season, hundreds of adults with their children go there for religious programs and recreation.

We soon saw that it would take a great deal of time to find the answer to our camping needs. Meanwhile, I entered into an agreement with the Y.M.C.A. camp, Camp Tochwogh, with the cooperation of Alva E. Lindley, the general secretary of the "Y". This camp was located on the Chesapeake near Betterton, Maryland. The "Y" loaned us the camp for five days each June before their program for the summer began. It was not nearly long enough, but we made the most of it, and it was a beginning. Children came from every parish and mission in the diocese. We emphasized worship—services were held in an attractive outdoor chapel. We also had the courses of instruction, as well as discussion groups. We sought to relate camping experience and nature study to religion.

One of the results of this was a new sense of companionship and solidarity among the young people of the diocese, which made for a stronger diocese. Youngsters took pride in feeling that they were a real part of the diocesan life and program. A vacuum had indeed been filled.

Some years later we were fortunate enough to secure Camp Arrowhead on Rehoboth Bay, a wonderful camp for boys which had been run by a retired Army colonel as a business proposition. When his health failed, he turned to the Episcopal church and he offered the facility to Diocese of Delaware for only $100,000. Where would the money come from?

Mr. Haskell was then chairman of the committee which had been appointed by me to find a permanent Delaware camp site. I invited Mr. Haskell to visit Camp Arrowhead with me and form an opinion about it. He was so enthusiastic about the camp that, at the end of the period of inspection, he took me to one side and said, "Bishop, this is it."

He told me, "Don't worry, Bishop. I'll see that the camp is given." I understand that Mr. Haskell, with the help of his friend, Governor Nelson Rockefeller of New York, paid the bill for this new camp.

The camp idea was accepted by the executive council and the convention, the generous offer of Mr. Haskell was also gratefully accepted, and soon we were in the camping business. I engaged professional camp people from Baltimore to take over the camp's operation.

Under the late Bishop William H. Mead, the camp has been promoted very effectively and has become a stronger factor in the life of the diocese. I firmly believe that if it is vigorously pushed the camp program will lead to more healthy and enthusiastic young people in the diocese.

During these exciting times, when things were moving and great decisions were being made, the executive council meetings were held each month at "Limerick", the charming home of Mr. and Mrs. Ellason Downs on Lancaster Pike. Mr. and Mrs. Downs had been elected to membership on the council and served for some time. I will never cease to doff my hat when I drive by that historic meeting place where so many great decisions were made. Molly Downs not only contributed delicious "goodies" for the "starving and unquenched" executive council members, but her wit and graciousness expedited the new program with a flourish and a grand effectiveness.

Robert N. Downs, III, was also a great addition to our number, and he saw to it that we not only discharged the important business of the executive council but that we had a good time. There was a great sense of joy and enthusiasm about the work.

I have often reflected on the secret of our Blessed Lord's influence over men while He worked upon this earth. It has seemed to me that he sought to lead and to govern by making them enthusiastic for the Kingdom. In our humble way, we tried to follow His example. In these days I worry about what I detect in the attitude of many people—I note a lack of enthusiasm that made our work in the Forties and Fifties so exciting and effective. So many people today apparently are so sophisticated as to have become quite negative. What they disbelieve far outweighs that which they profess to believe. If Satan can persuade Christians to become repudiators, then he renders us ineffective followers of Christ. So many people know too much for one person but not enough for two. There are so many among us who have become so open-minded that their minds are open at both ends. Their enthusiasm has fallen out, and sometimes their brains too!

Positive thinking coined by a prominent New York parson has been scoffed at as being both naive and silly. I do not here intend to endorse Doctor Vincent Peale—I have very little knowledge of what he has had to say. Though it may be thought smart by extremists today to deny and to scoff at the principles that once brought life and zeal into our Christian life and belief, I do remember the saying of that famous man, Nietzsche, who once wrote, "If a man looks long enough into the abyss, the abyss will surely look into him."

Programs and budgets are fine, useful and necessary, but they amount to very little unless there is a vital spirit of faith in the leadership of each congregation. We need a daily Pentecost! We indeed need to believe that our God is a God of miracles—a God of wonders, and to follow Him!

[147]

Chapter 18

A New Bishopstead

By the mid 1940's, I could truthfully say many things were beginning to percolate in this old diocese. There was a quickened momentum felt throughout the state, typified by a proposal, made to me following a routine meeting of the trustees, that the diocese sell the old Bishopstead on Fourteenth Street and secure a new one.

It was explained to me that the area around Bishopstead was deteriorating rapidly and that we would be wise to find a new location. Macmillan Hoopes reminded me that this would be quite possible under the deed of gift, of the late Francis G. du Pont, providing the Bishop of Delaware agreed. The old Bishopstead had never been quite sound after a Du Pont powder wagon explosion in 1858 had damaged the structure.

Knowing something of the history of Bishopstead, and because Bishop Alfred Lee's granddaughters still lived in Delaware, I was a little timid about talking to people about this proposed change. However, I found that the granddaughters of Bishop Lee had no hesitation whatsoever. They were most gracious and understanding.

For many weeks thereafter we looked for a new Bishopstead, and I was taken to some enormous mansions which I found to be unexceptable. Finally the Reverend Doctor Charles L. Candee, pastor of Westminster Presbyterian Church, and now retired, came to me and said, "Bishop, my wife and I drove down Fourteenth Street last

New Bishopstead

The Chapel at Bishopstead

night, past Bishopstead, and we noted the many changes that have taken place in that neighborhood. My wife said to me, 'Let us find the Bishop a better place to live in!' "

After I had confided in him the conclusions of the board of trustees. Doctor Candee asked: "Will you appoint me a committee of one to find you a new Bishopstead?" I readily agreed, and he went to work.

In two or three days, he called me and asked me to meet him at 2 p.m. at a certain corner—he had a place in mind. He took me past the Delaware Art Center to the top of the hill. There stood the unoccupied and magnificent home of the late Joseph Bancroft.

This home had been constructed seventy-five years earlier. Legend has it that it took a full year to blast the basement out of solid granite, and four years to complete the house itself. The house was built of hammered gray granite with two granite windows and door trim. Its architecture was an adaptation of country English Tudor style. It had thirteen rooms, including eight bedrooms and five bathrooms. There was a glass-walled conservatory.

At the east end of the house was a wide covered porch that was accessible to both the study and its adjacent living room. At the back of the house was a flagstone terrace. A grape-vine had been planted in the conservatory—grown from a cutting of a vine planted at Hampton Court, England, by King Henry the Eighth. On the first floor was a broad reception room with paneled oak walls. The property comprised about three or four acres was graced by beautiful woods and shrubbery. (After the diocese purchased the place, the late Mrs. Alfred I. du Pont made it possible to purchase the rest of the hillside beyond the original property.) The late Mr. Bancroft was a great lover of nature and he had carefully and expertly planted his trees and shrubs. . . as well as a hardy azalea hedge, fifteen feet high and a hundred feet long. There were also many rhododendrons and a magnificent row of laurel.

It was decided to purchase this property after

Mrs. Irenee du Pont and the late A. Felix du Pont (whose father, the late Francis G. du Pont, had donated old Bishopstead) had enthusiastically approved the project. Felix du Pont told the trustees that money would be provided for the purchase of the property and for the complete renovation of the house. He also insisted that the highly revered chapel be removed from Bishopstead, that it be taken down, brick by brick, and carefully reassembled on the new site next to the conservatory.

The entire cost of the property, including the transporting of the chapel, was borne by gifts from Mrs. Irenee du Pont and her brother, Felix. And when they had made this provision, they added, with that wonderful candidness with which some people are endowed, "When the old Bishopstead property is sold, you will please put the money into a fund to help maintain the new one."

In mid 1945, the Bishop and his family moved into the new Bishopstead. It was perfect in every way, a wonderful place for entertaining people. Two of our daughters were married in the chapel.

[151]

The lean, troublesome years—years of stringency and anxiety—were behind us. The annual lay conference which met at St. Andrew's School each September had succeeded in galvanizing the laity into a new and expectant attitude. There was a feeling of diocesan fellowship and trust abroad. Bridges had been built between southern Delaware and New Castle County and Wilmington.

A revived sense of Christian stewardship was beginning to show in every section of the diocese, bringing in generous, unsolicited gifts each year-end in addition to the pledged support of the people in each parish. We seemed to be on our way. The survey had given us a track on which to run. It was time to be thinking of other things that would help to expedite and widen our horizons still more. And one of these projects, I felt, must be the introduction of rotation for the office of vestryman.

During the Second World War, I went up and

down the diocese, preaching that when our young men came back from the war we must find places for them on our vestries.

Until that time, the vestries had been closed corporations. Vestrymen re-elected themselves and served until they died. I had a feeling that we needed to give young men of ability and dedication a chance to serve on parish vestries. In order to bring about rotation in the office of vestrymen it was necessary to make a change in the constitution of the diocese. I proposed this and even suggested the text of the change. The amendment to the constitution would provide for a three-year term for a vestryman. A man would not be able to succeed himself until he had been off the vestry for a year at least.

It took a powerful lot of oratory on my part to get any consideration of this change. I knew there was great opposition to it on the part of conservative vestrymen and church members.

I was able to get the change in the constitution ratified on its first reading at a convention which met in St. Andrew's Church in Wilmington. It rather squeaked by, but with a sufficient number of votes to register the prospect of a change.

A year later, the convention met at the Church of the Ascension, in Claymont. Once more I referred to the matter in my address to the convention and urged the delegates to complete the change in the constitution by voting for it a second time.

The matter was up for discussion. Slowly, Richard S. Rodney, federal judge and senior warden of Immanuel Church, New Castle, much admired and respected, rose to speak. He said, "Bishop, I hesitate to speak against anything that you, personally, want."

I asked pardon for interrupting the judge and addressed the delegates: "Gentlemen, never express that attitude on the floor of this convention. Speak your mind. Vote your conscience. I have explained to you why I think the rotation in the office of vestryman would be good for this diocese. I have also told you that I myself am a convert to the idea. When I was rector of St. Paul's in Albany a prominent vestryman, there, suggested this plan. I declined. I would not think of changing wonderful vestrymen for unknown men. But, when I went to St. Mark's Church, San Antonio, as a rector, I found rotation in office already in vogue there. I was amazed at what it had done for that parish. Instead of twelve or fifteen well informed men serving on the vestry year after year, there were now nearly seventy men who were informed, knowledgeable and well equipped to serve on the vestry. It made a great difference in that parish's life."

Then I turned to Judge Rodney and I politely urged him to proceed.

The judge said he disliked the mandatory aspect of the change. He didn't like the idea of every vestry falling in line, in lock-step precision, by a certain date the next year—introducing rotation according to the proposed law of the diocese. He went on to say, "I haven't the slightest doubt that if I should introduce a resolution stating that at the first convenient moment in the life of a parish, rotation be adopted—I haven't the slightest doubt that it would pass unanimously."

The judge then sat, but his remarks had been so persuasive I could see the other delegates nodding in agreement. At the vote, my measure was defeated.

Quickly I rose and said, "Now, Judge Rodney, you may introduce your resolution." The judge looked rather surprised and asked, "What resolution?"

I said, "The last vote taken was predicated on your suggestion that you were going to introduce a resolution requiring each parish to adopt rotation of office at its earliest possible convenience."

The judge was a little flustered, "Well, yes. Yes, I will introduce that resolution." He did and it was carried. I felt that I had won a great victory.

When I adjourned the session for lunch, the Reverend Richard W. Trapnell, then rector at Middletown, dashed up to me and said, "Bishop, you've thrown the baby out with the wash."

I said, "No, Dick, you know as well as I do you cannot drive Delaware people. But you can lead them, and I will see to it that the convenient moment comes very quickly in each of the parishes."

I was able to do just that. Within a remarkably short time, rotation in office was the accepted rule throughout the diocese and it began to make tremendous improvements in the number of men and women who were able to serve their churches. I consider rotation in office for vestrymen one of the great achievements of my ministry in Delaware. It opened the door to many new and able men and women who were anxious to serve the church.

Chapter 19

Early Ecumenical Experiences

As Bishop of Delaware, I had to, of course, give the diocese my first efforts. However, there were also other community matters having to do with Christianity that deserved attention. I soon learned that the clergy of other non-Roman communions were exceedingly courteous and responsive. I had always been active in Christian work involving other churches. The subject of my senior class oration in Chanute, Kansas, in the spring of 1914 had been Christian unity and how it may be achieved. This essay won the gold medal at that commencement, long before any thought of an ecumenical movement. Some of the people who heard my remarks thought I was bit weird and unorthodox.

Early in my ministry in Delaware I worked with other clergymen in the reorganization of the Wilmington Council of Churches. I was delighted to work with such clerics as the Reverend Doctor Benjamin Johns, of Grace Methodist Church, the Reverend Doctor Albert H. Kleffman of West Presbyterian Church, the Reverend F. Raymond Baker, the Reverend Doctor John W. Christie and others, including Alva E. Lindley, executive secretary of the YMCA in Wilmington.

We all began to dream for the day when we might have a full-time executive secretary heading up the Wilmington Council of Churches. That day dawned sooner than we expected, since we were able to call Wilbert Smith, who had retired from the international service of the YMCA, to fill the post. He was a remarkable man of great understanding, wisdom and world-wide experience in Christian work. I took every opportunity as president of the Council to assist the movement, and I rejoiced over its results.

I was fortunate in having happy and friendly contacts with almost all of the state's churches and religious groups. Some of my most wonderful experiences were at Quaker meetings and in dealings with members of the Friends. Incidentally, one of my grandmothers was reared a Quaker.

One of the interesting experiences in this general field of Christian cooperation involved Doctor Christie and myself at a Good Friday service in Laurel, Delaware. I had returned to Delaware in mid-February of 1943 after many weeks in Florida, where I'd been recovering from the heart exhaustion of the past October.

One day, following an inter-denominational service at St. Andrew's Church, I had been lunching with several of the parsons of other churches. At this luncheon, Doctor Christie spoke: "Bishop, did I read in the papers that you are going to conduct what you Episcopalians call the Three-Hour Service somewhere downstate on Good Friday?"

I replied I had promised to conduct such a service at St. Philip's Episcopal Church in Laurel on Good Friday, lasting from noon until 3 p.m. Doctor Christie wanted to know how many addresses I would give. I told him and the others I would give seven addresses based on the seven words from the Cross, and one introductory address—a total of eight.

Doctor Christie exploded, "You have no business doing a thing of this kind; you've been quite ill."

The other clergy present were bent on discussing

other matters but Doctor Christie could not get his mind off my proposed trip to Laurel on Good Friday. Eventually he offered to drive me to Laurel and back on that day. "At least you won't have to put out any energy driving your car," he said.

I thanked him sincerely but reminded him that he was the pastor of a great congregation in Wilmington and could scarcely be spared on the eve of Easter.

He said, "I intend to be with you on that day." Then he added, "Bishop, this may be preposterous from your point of view, but will you let me give half of those addresses on Good Friday?"

The other men instantly fell silent and fixed their eyes on me. I could almost hear their thinking at that moment: "This Bishop has been doing a lot of preaching about Christian unity. Here's a chance for him to endorse what he says by his deeds."

I addressed Doctor Christie: "That is the most kind and considerate offer you have ever made, and I gratefully accept it." I could sense a feeling of relief around the table.

I went back to my office at the Cathedral a bit heavy-hearted. I knew I had to deal with a rather strict rector in Laurel, the Reverend Robert Y. Barber. In 1943, interchurch cooperation, at least to the extent of worship services, was not generally the rule—certainly not in that area of the state.

I telephoned the rector and said to him, "Now look, 'Father' Barber, you often talk to me, and to your congregation as well, about the importance of following the leadership of the Holy Spirit. Now I am going to report something to you which I really feel has the leadership of the Holy Spirit. I am going to share with you exactly how it happened, and how it developed."

Then I told him about Doctor Christie's proposal. I said I felt I could do nothing but accept, and I thought it was magnificent of Doctor Christie to make the offer.

Reverend Barber responded by shouting, "I do not want him."

I asked why he felt that way and he replied, "It's Good Friday."

"Well," I said, "I never knew that the Episcopal Church had a monopoly on Good Friday."

The rector stammered a bit and said, "Of course we don't have a monopoly."

I proceeded to puncture his argument further by saying I had read in the papers that he intended to have an inter-denominational service in Laurel earlier in Holy Week. I asked what the difference was? "Besides," I said, "our Three-Hour Service on Good Friday is not a liturgical service. It's not found in the prayer book, after all."

Again the rector muttered, "I do not want him."

"Very well," I said. "You leave me only one thing to do. I will have to phone the Reverend Doctor Christie, the pastor of the important Westminster Presbyterian Church in Wilmington, and tell him that you, the rector, refuse to let him officiate with me in your church on Good Friday."

There was a period of silence, after which the rector said, "All right, you bring him. We'll go through with it."

I asked him, "Are you sure?"

Rather faintly he replied, "Yes. Good-bye."

Doctor Christie and I were half-way downstate when he took his eyes off the road and asked anxiously, "By the way, Bishop, the rector at Laurel wants me, doesn't he?"

I replied as a true diplomat, "Oh, he is expecting you."

When we arrived at Laurel, I took Doctor Christie at once through a back door to a classroom in the parish house, not far from the official vesting room. I explained to him he would vest in that particular room and I would come back for him when the service was ready to begin. I had asked him to bring his black cassock, his white Geneva bib—which some people thought was a bit high church—and also to wear his doctor's silk gown which he ordinarily wore in his church. I closed the door so no one would be tempted to engage him in conversation, and perhaps "spill the beans".

In the vesting room, I put on my rather simple purple cassock. Meanwhile, the chancel door was open and I could hear conversations in the church. The rector saying to some dear old soul, "Guess what our Bishop has gone and done now." He proceeded, "Believe it or not, he has brought a Presbyterian minister with him to take part in this Good Friday Service."

I could almost hear the clucking of tongues.

The time came for the service to begin and I fetched Doctor Christie. Together we went into the church. Doctor Christie looked a bit more like the Bishop [159] and I, the curate. His preaching was as fine as I have listened to anywhere. The people of St. Philip's were thrilled and, I might say, enthralled by his preaching. I took my share of the addresses and conducted the Prayer Service.

After three o'clock when the service was ended, Father Barber embraced us both and with sincere affection took us to the rectory, where he fed us well and sent us off to Wilmington with enthusiastic praise and thanks. It was a miracle.

The news of this service, the first of its kind in Delaware, spread all over Sussex County, and even over the whole state. Some hidebound literalists, I am sure, were shocked by the antics of the Bishop, but the overall effect was very stimulating. I never told Doctor Christie about this ridiculous situation until many years later, and when I did he nearly died laughing.

Long after, when Doctor Christie's wonderful

wife was seriously ill, I had an opportunity to partially repay my friend in kind.

I said to him at a luncheon, "John, I hear you are going to the Methodist Church in Seaford to preach on Wednesday evening in Holy Week."

Doctor Christie allowed as how that was correct. Then I said, remembering his words some years before, "John, you have no business doing this. You have a lot on your mind; your wife has been very ill. I'll drive you down to Seaford and back."

When we got to the Seaford church, I reminded Doctor Christie that he must not tell the pastor, the Reverend Doctor Stone, that I was in the congregation at the back of the church, hiding out. I merely wanted to worship quietly and to listen to a good sermon. He reluctantly promised he would be good. When the sermon was over and during the taking of the offering, I saw John Christie whispering into the pastor's ear. Instantly Doctor Stone came down the side aisle, looking for me.

He invited me to the platform to pronounce the benediction. And so I accompanied him back to the clergy stalls and sat between him and Doctor Christie. At the proper time I was presented to the congregation and gave the benediction. Then before the organist could begin the inevitable postlude, Doctor Christie jumped up and asked the congregation, "Where else in the whole country would you find an Episcopal Bishop driving a Presbyterian parson a hundred miles, down-state and back, to enable the Presbyterian to preach in a Methodist Church?"

There was general laughter throughout the church. The congregation went forward and shook hands with the pastor, the special preacher and the Bishop.

I do not believe it is too much to say that the two events which I have here chronicled had their effect in Delaware. From my earliest days in the state, I had preached quite often in Westminster Presbyterian

Church, Wilmington, St. Stephen's Church, and in other churches in the area. I always opened and closed the St. Andrew's interdenominational Lenten Services, Ash Wednesday and Maundy Thursday, and in those days the congregations filled St. Andrew's to overflowing. Often there were chairs in the crypt underneath the sanctuary and people standing in the nave.

I used to invite Protestant clergy to Bishopstead one day each autumn when we would worship together in the chapel, listen to an inspiring guest speaker and, after that, lunch together on the lawn.

Beginning in Albany, New York, I had been a substitute preacher on occasion in the temple of the Reform Jewish congregation near my parish church. Whenever the rabbi was sick they would send for me. And when I moved to San Antonio, Rabbi Frish, who was the pastor of the Reform congregation in that city, having heard of my contacts with the Albany congregation, would call on me in emergencies.

In Wilmington, Rabbi Henry Tavel of Temple Beth Emeth and I were very dear friends; he facetiously called me his "Bishop". When he was succeeded by Rabbi Herbert E. Drooz, who had been a teenager in the Albany temple congregation, I took part in his installation in the old temple on Washington Street near Ninth.

I was never invited to officiate in any Roman Catholic church in Delaware, although Father J. Francis Tucker and I were very dear friends from the very beginning of my life in Wilmington. He always told audiences, when we were on the platform together, that his mother had been the seamstress to the wife of the second Bishop of Delaware, Leighton Coleman. During my earlier days at old Bishopstead, whenever he heard of illness in the family, he immediately came to call.

Father Tucker was transferred from St. Anthony's Church in Wilmington to Rome, and later to St. Charles' Church in Monaco, where he was also chaplain to Prince Rainier and Princess Grace. He is credited with skillfully promoting that romance. When he came back to Wilmington for visits, I always tried to get him to have dinner at Bishopstead. When I succeeded, I invited many of my friends for the evening and we had a gala.

I think Father Tucker was really one of the original ecumenical advocates in the Roman Catholic Church. For instance, when King George VI died, Father Tucker called from his rectory to ask the Bishop under whom he served for permission to hold a memorial service in St. Charles' Church, Monaco, honoring the late King George. He explained to the Bishop that there were many English and American people in Monaco who would appreciate it. Father Tucker later told me the Bishop bluntly refused, saying, "You know very well, Father Tucker, that the late English monarch was a Protestant."

[162]

Father Tucker was very much provoked. Later, the Bishop phoned back. Possibly he had been influenced by the Prince and Princess of Monaco, or maybe he had called Rome and received permission. At any rate, within a short time he phoned again saying: "This is your Bishop speaking. It has just occurred to me to order you to hold a memorial service at St. Charles' Church on Wednesday morning at eleven o'clock, in honor of the late King of England. I will be present to pontificate. And, oh yes, Father Tucker, I will take care of all the publicity for the service myself. Good-bye."

Father Tucker was delegated to the job of lighting candles. He was furious with the Bishop. When he told me the story he wound up by saying in disgust, "The old goat."

While Father Tucker was still rector at St. Anthony's, he invited the Reverend Alex W. Boyer, then our rector at Newport, to assist in the wedding service in which his brother was being married to one of the girls of St. Anthony's parish.

Father Tucker returned from Europe to Wilmington to spend the rest of his days here. Upon his sixtieth anniversary of ordination there was a great service in St. Anthony's Church. He insisted, and the Bishop of the Diocese of Wilmington agreed, that I should be vested. In the procession I was assigned a prominent seat in the sanctuary of the church, attended by two chaplains. The Bishop of Wilmington came across the sanctuary to me at a certain point in the service and gave me the kiss of peace, after which I was honored by the censors swinging the incense in my direction.

Chapter 20

Extra-Diocesan Activities

Not long after I became Bishop of Delaware, I realized I could not continue to dodge responsibilities beyond the diocesan boundary lines.

In 1943, the Right Reverend Henry K. Sherrill, the great Bishop of Massachusetts and also chairman of the Army and Navy Commission of the Episcopal Church, invited me to meet him in Philadelphia for a conference. He explained to me at the conference that the commission needed to raise a million dollars for Episcopal chaplains and their ministry to fellow churchmen in the armed forces.

Bishop Sherrill asked me to become the executive chairman of the commission and to be responsible for raising the funds and conducting the campaign. While I listened to his arguments, I recalled that only two or three weeks before, the Right Reverend Henry St. George Tucker, then our Presiding Bishop told me he intended to resign his post at the next General Convention. He had held this position since 1937. I had asked him if he had given any thought to his possible successor. Bishop Tucker replied that the only man he could see for the post was Bishop Sherrill.

That was good enough for me. I had assisted Doctor Sherrill in 1920 on Easter at his church in Longwood, Massachusetts, at the time I was a student in Cambridge. After he had been elected the Bishop of Massachusetts, following his great ministry at Trinity Church, Boston, he had visited my parish in Albany, coming to preach during a Lenten season. I thought him a wonderful person, and I found myself often asking myself, when faced with a puzzling problem in Delaware, "What would Henry do about this?"

So as I talked with Bishop Sherrill in Philadelphia early in 1943, I kept saying to myself, "This is the man Bishop Tucker thinks should be the next Presiding Bishop."

I also knew that Bishop Sherrill was totally ignorant about Bishop Tucker's thought on this. Through the years, Bishop Sherrill had stuck so conscientiously to his duties in Massachusetts that he had never roamed very much around the church. Therefore, I sincerely doubted the church in the south, in the midwest or the far west, appreciated the gifts of the Bishop of Massachusetts.

I found myself thinking—if I accepted Bishop Sherrill's appointment I could present him to the church on a "fool-proof" itinerary where engagements would be set-up under favorable conditions. At the same time we could raise the money so desperately needed for our chaplains in World War II. Hopefully, Bishop Sherrill would consent to make addresses throughout the church on the subject of the Army and Navy Commission.

[165]

Therefore, I countered with two stipulations: first, I asked if I might have offices at the most popular address in the Episcopal Church at that time; namely, the Church Pension Fund, which was located at 20 Exchange Place in New York; and second, I requested a free hand in the selection of our campaign manager and his staff. He agreed to these proposals, and I accepted my assignment.

The Church Pension Fund eagerly cooperated and placed offices at our disposal. I convinced the Reverend Dr. David Covell, secretary of the Forward Movement Commission in Cincinnati, to come east and run the campaign. We were in business!

I commuted to Wall Street at least once a week

for conferences with Doctor Covell. Together we sent Bishop Sherrill throughout the church, speaking on a subject very close to his heart and to ours; namely, the needed pastoral care of the Episcopalians serving in the armed forces. His itinerary was far-flung and well handled. He made friends everywhere he went. I devoutly hoped that while we appealed to the church to give us the funds we needed, Bishop Sherrill would at the same time make such a deep impression on the whole church they would instinctively think of him as the next Presiding Bishop.

Fully expecting Bishop Tucker to retire at the Cleveland convention, we had taken into our confidence seven other Bishops in the provinces of the church. We told them what Bishop Tucker had said about Bishop Sherrill, asking them to keep this confidential. My purpose was to alert them to the possibility of "favorite sons" in their areas.

I felt these must be convinced that Bishop Sherrill was really the logical choice for Presiding Bishop. So, every time a favorite son showed his head, I looked over the list of Bishops and requested the Bishop closest to the favorite son to go and have a heart to heart talk with him. Bishop Tucker took us by surprise when, in Cleveland, his friends persuaded him to stay on three more years.

My cooperating seven Bishops merely kept their eyes and ears open. We continued with our delicate little technique until the time of the convention in 1946. Bishop Sherrill was nominated for the post, as were one or two other Bishops; but Bishop Sherrill, now so widely known and respected, was elected on the first ballot. Through all this, he never knew anything about what I was up to. I felt justified in doing what I did toward prompting his election because I respected Bishop Tucker's judgment, and I knew in my own heart that the Bishop of Massachusetts was the outstanding man for the position.

Also in 1946, I was elected to the National

Council as a member of that body. It must be noted that the name of the Council has now been changed to the National Executive Council.

One of the first things I was able to do for the new Presiding Bishop was to assist him in the purchase of Seabury House, outside Greenwich. This property had belonged to the late Mr. Satterly, a brother-in-law of J. P. Morgan, the elder. The property was now for sale at a ridiculously low price. It consisted of forty acres or more. There were great orchards, gardens and beautiful trees and a really great mansion. On the property were several other residences including one beautiful home which could be used as the residence for the Presiding Bishop of the church.

Bishop Sherrill was very timid about his ability to raise $100,000 to buy the property. I stuck with him, insisting that he try. At one point he was ready to give up the whole project. But I coaxed him to come to Wilmington and I introduced him to Mrs. Alfred I. du Pont, among others. She gladly gave him his first $10,000 towards the amount needed. The money was raised and the property has been the proud possession of the Episcopal Church ever since. Today it is worth certainly over a million dollars.

Another general church assignment given to me in 1949 was the chairmanship of a special committee appointed by the Presiding Bishop to try to defeat the efforts of a New Mexico churchman, who was obsessed with the notion that the entire assets of the Church Pension Fund should be invested in common stocks. The economy in 1949 was not stable. People were not sure what was going to happen. The experts in Wall Street, and those in charge of the Church Pension Fund, were dubious about the prospect of investing all assets in common stocks. At that time I doubt there was more than twenty-five per cent of the pension fund invested in common stocks—the remainder was invested in good, safe bonds and preferred stocks. I fought valiantly through the church press, and at the General Convention in 1949, to defeat the proposal made by the churchman from New Mexico. We succeeded in defeating his proposal.

The disappointed man asked my brother-in-law, the Reverend R. Y. Davis, a missionary to the Navajo Indians, "Why is your brother-in-law, the Bishop of Delaware, so mean to me?"

Looking back on that fight from the vantage point of the year 1974, I must say that if the church had followed the advice of the rancher from New Mexico, the pension fund today would possibly be double its present size. But who could have known for sure? We had not yet completely recovered from the difficulties and strains of the Second World War by the time the General Convention met in 1949.

At the General Convention of 1967 in Seattle, it was decided the Church Pension Fund be empowered to invest a larger proportion of the fund in common stocks. But who can tell, even now, whether this will prove to be wise? It is possible I helped the church to miss the boat. However, at that time everyone knowledgeable in the field of investments felt we were doing the right thing for the safety of the fund—more especially because we did not wish to endanger the pensions and retirement allowances granted to disabled or retired clergy and their dependents.

I served on the National Council for six years, through 1952. By this time bad health had begun to have its effect. I nearly died in October 1942 from heart exhaustion brought on by an improvident use of my strength. From this I gradually recovered. In 1947 I had been the victim of a severe case of infectious jaundice, which nearly finished me. Incidentally, I picked-up that disease in a doctor's office in Corpus Christi, Texas, where I had gone for a simple cold injection. By 1951, I discovered I had gall stones and, a year later, I developed diabetes.

One of my general church contacts was as a

member of the Chapter of the Washington Cathedral in Washington, D.C. (such a chapter is something like a vestry in a parish church—the governing body). I think I must have been elected to the chapter around 1945.

Over the years I developed a very keen interest in the Cathedral. If the architect's plans were to be carried out, according to published intentions, I believed the Washington Cathedral would ultimately be the most beautiful church edifice in the United States, and one of the most beautiful in the entire world.

Also I was enthusiastic about the educational program of the Cathedral. Of course, the Cathedral has been, from the very beginning, a church of worship for all people. It is most fitting that it should be on the highest hill in the city of Washington and available to religious people of all persuasions.

First of all, there is the College of Preachers, which was built and endowed during the episcopate of Bishop James E. Freeman. This is a college for men in the active ministry who desire to come back for study and for refresher courses. There is also the famous National Cathedral School for Girls, the St. Alban's School for Boys, and Belvoir School for Little Children. All of these are owned by the Cathedral Chapter.

The Cathedral Chapter met once each month except for the summer months of July and August. I recall some of my fellow members on the chapter; the Right Reverend Angus Dun, Bishop of Washington, presided. Next to me always sat George Wharton Pepper, once United States senator from Pennsylvania, and one of the greatest churchmen in the United States. Across the table was Junius Morgan, of the House of Morgan, New York. There were also Mr. Robert Fleming, the president of the Riggs Bank in Washington; Clifford Folger, another banker; and Harold Rust, a splendid businessman also from Washington. There were many others, but these were the ones I encountered most often.

Senator Pepper and I always sat side by side near

Bishop Dun. Several times the senator and I took stands that were ultimately of considerable importance. For example, one of the greatest boosters of the Cathedral was a James Sheldon of New York City. Mr. Sheldon loved the Cathedral with a real and passionate devotion. He was always proposing things which he thought would be of interest or of benefit to the Cathedral grounds. Several of these proposals aroused the ire of Bishop Dun. On one occasion Bishop Dun reported to the chapter that he intended to write Mr. Sheldon and tell him bluntly that his help was not required and we would all be happy if he would leave the Cathedral alone.

Senator Pepper and I, aided by Junius Morgan across the table, urged caution in dealing with Mr. Sheldon, pointing out that the man was devoted to the Cathedral. We proposed that the Bishop request the dean at that time, John Sutter, to go to New York and palaver with Mr. Sheldon. Dean Sutter was very successful in his missions and things remained calm for a while longer.

The final blowup almost came when Mr. Sheldon asked for permission to provide a large equestrian statue of George Washington astride his steed—the work to be done by a famous French sculptor. He wanted this bit of art to be placed well below the Pilgrim's Steps on the south side. The suggestion that almost finished Bishop Dun was Mr. Sheldon's desire to have the statue covered with gold leaf. Again we prevailed upon the Bishop to keep his temper and show a little caution. We proposed he send an emissary to New York to talk to Mr. Sheldon. We were able to get over this crisis in a satisfactory way, and Bishop Dun showed remarkably good statesmanship, as well as good sportsmanship, when he permitted Mr. Sheldon to go ahead with his proposal. As a matter of fact, while none of us would want such a work of art in his own living room, it does not seem out of place, certainly as one looks at it with the great Cathedral as a background.

The point I wish to make is this. When James Sheldon died, he left his entire fortune to the Cathedral, and the chapter of the Cathedral was able to keep building on Mr. Sheldon's money for a good many years.

In recent years, the work of construction of the Cathedral has gone forward with great rapidity. The south transept and the south entrance were completed. The glorious great central tower has been built; this houses magnificent chimes and bells. The side aisles of the nave have been erected, and the nave is extensive—including the beginning of the West Towers. One of these will be called the Winston Churchill Memorial Tower. I pray devoutly that the people of the church will respond to the appeal for funds for this tower. It is, I am sure, too much for me to hope to see the completion of the Churchill Tower, but I can hope!

In 1948, when my wife, Isabelle, and I were in London, my cousin, Sir Archibald McKinstry and his wife, Lady Sarah, arranged for us to be among the first civilians to visit and inspect the deep caverns, well below the surface of the earth and the Ministry of Defense Building in London. From there Churchill directed England's war effort in the Second World War.

In those dark days, the whole world feared for England's life. We were told about the terrible times the guards had to prevent Churchill from rushing out of doors as soon as he heard the attacking German airplanes overhead. It was almost impossible to keep him indoors. He would stalk out, shake his fists at the planes, and remain outside to see what was going on.

During our visit to the underground rooms from which the war was directed, we were shown the tiny broadcast booth from which Churchill made his world-stirring addresses. For example, when he spoke about the necessity of the English to fight the enemy, he cried, "We will fight them in the air. We will fight them on the beaches." We were told that, at that point in his address he put his hand over the microphone and said to a few intimates in the broadcast booth, "We will hit them over the head with beer bottles—that's about all we've got." Then he proceeded with his extraordinary address to the world. I remember it so well because I was en route to Valley Forge at the time the speech was given, and I became so enthralled by its eloquence and its boldness that I nearly ran off the road.

Winston Churchill, despite any ambitious detractors, certainly was the greatest statesman in my lifetime and should ever be remembered for keeping the spark of freedom alive in our darkest hour. It is for this reason that the Washington Cathedral intends to memorialize him by erecting a great tower which will be higher even than the Washington Monument. It is my hope certainly that the Cathedral will be successful in arousing the interest of the churchmen of Delaware, and the country, in the support of this project. Fortunately, Delaware's very strong and alert National Cathedral Association will almost certainly make this one of their projects.

When I retired from the active ministry for health reasons, I most reluctantly resigned from the Cathedral Chapter. One of the things I did while a member was to nominate Miss Katherine Lee, an old San Antonio friend and former headmistress of several important schools, to be headmistress of the National Cathedral School for Girls. She served in a marvelous way as headmistress for sixteen years. She retired with the commencement of 1967. I am very proud of my part in persuading her to go to the National Cathedral School. I believe Miss Lee was the most effective headmistress the school has ever had.

Chapter 21

An American Bishop
in London

In the summer of 1948, I had the privilege of representing the Diocese of Delaware at Lambeth Conference, held at Lambeth Palace, London, the home of the Archbishop of Canterbury, the spiritual head of the Anglican Communion. I had always remembered the report made by my Bishop in Kansas, James A. Wise, who had attended the 1920 Lambeth Conference. He had greatly impressed me with the details of his summer in London. Of course, Lambeth 1920 was quite different from Lambeth 1948.

I had never been abroad and looked forward to my visit to England with great excitement. By rights, the conference should have been held in 1940, because it was an occasion which took place every ten years. But the Second World War had postponed the opening of Lambeth until 1948.

When my friend, the Right Reverend Frank A. Juhan, Bishop of Florida, wrote me in December of 1947 to ask if I thought it wise for me to go to Lambeth in view of my recent illness—a serious attack of infectious jaundice which had taken place the summer of 1947—I replied of course I would go to Lambeth, although I still was inconvenienced by an aching liver. Naturally, I would take my wife with me. That settled, we began to make our plans accordingly.

In the early part of 1948, both the Juhans and

the McKinstrys had received letters from Mrs. Alfred I. du Pont, asking if we would seriously object if she went along to London with us. Of course, she wouldn't be attending Lambeth Conference, since her aim was to have a good time with her many friends in England. We assured her that we would love to have her come along. She then wrote back, saying, in a very off-hand way, that she would be pleased if we would let her make the reservations at a London hotel, inasmuch as she knew the ropes very well. We told her we would be very happy for her to do this. Secretly I worried about the cost of any hospitality which she might engage for us, but I decided to take a chance. Before Mrs. McKinstry and I sailed on the Mauretania in mid-June 1948, ahead of Mrs. du Pont and the Juhans, we were informed by her that we would all register at Claridge's on a late June day just prior to the opening of Lambeth Conference at Canterbury Cathedral. (I had no idea at that time that Claridge's was the most expensive hotel in the world and probably the most regal. Many illustrious people were staying at Claridge's during our six weeks there, including the Shah of Iran and his first wife.)

I was scheduled to join a small group of American Bishops in Scotland prior to the Lambeth Conference to dedicate a memorial to the memory of the first American Bishop to be consecrated by Scottish Bishops in Aberdeen. So we arrived in London a week or ten days ahead of our friends. We had spent our first few days in London at Grosvenor House, and we did not go over to Claridge's to inspect it until we got back from Scotland. Then we moved into that elaborate hostel the day before our friends arrived.

The manager of Claridge's, dressed in cutaway and striped trousers, conducted us personally to our "suite". Our eyes were wide in a combination of wonder and fear.

"Isn't there some mistake?" I asked. "Isn't this

suite reserved for Bishop and Mrs. Juhan and for Mrs. du Pont?"

The manager assured us the suite was for the McKinstrys. The Juhans and Mrs. du Pont had suites farther down the hall, he said. Well—what luxury! What would be the cost of all this?

In a state of near panic, we left our rooms for dinner. The main dining room was also on a grand scale. We charged our wonderful dinner to our suite, and then, returning to our rooms once more to consider our peril (or good fortune—we didn't know which) we found that the maids had unpacked our bags in our absence. They had also set out my long white Bishop's rochet (vestment) with its puffy sleeves—for my wife's nightie. Bishop's sleeves were quite the thing in those days.

I slept very little that first night, wondering how I would ever pay for six weeks of such luxury. I was really almost half sick over the thought and yet too timid to confront the impressive and forbidding people at the hotel desk to demand of them "How much?" Before we could conceive of a plan of escape to a moderately priced hotel, the Juhans and Mrs. du Pont arrived and we had a most happy reunion in our "suite".

[175]

Mrs. du Pont had an invitation for dinner "out" that night, leaving the Juhans and the McKinstrys to their own devices. We had dinner in the main dining room. At the end of the delicious dinner, I asked Bishop Juhan if he would like a Havana cigar. He said he would. So I ordered some.

A waiter came with a jewel-box-type affair, which he carefully unlocked in our presence, pulling back the curved-cover top and revealing Churchillian-sized cigars from Havana. We each took one.

I said, "Put it on the bill," and signed for the cigars.

The low bows of the waiter who had brought us the cigars aroused my suspicion, and I called him back and asked him, "How much?" He replied, "Four dollars each, sir."

The next morning, I could be seen sneaking across the street to a little modest tobacco shop where I bought some cheap cigars. Havana cigars were still under war taxes.

Our life at Claridge's was quite exciting. Many nights we went to the 6 p.m. theater unless there was some other engagement which was more pressing, and this theater experience was followed by a late ten o'clock dinner at Claridge's. Breakfast was brought into our bedroom every morning promptly at eight. We had numerous dinner parties. Among our most interesting guests were Lord and Lady Astor. I found Lady Astor to be one of the most amusing persons I have ever seen and known. When she entered the main dining room on my arm, the entire assemblage rose in her honor; an American woman who had made good! We had many of our American Bishops and their wives to our dinners.

The opening service at Canterbury Cathedral was an occasion which will never be forgotten by me. The Archbishop, Doctor Fischer, presided. He was most appealing to me; friendly, frank, democratic, with a keen sense of humor. He always seemed more like an American than an Englishman. His directness of dealing was revealed to me in one particular incident.

Midway through the Lambeth sessions, the Anglican Bishops had been discussing the advisability of sending a delegation to call on the Russian Orthodox Bishops in Russia. The purpose of the visit would be to compliment the Russian Church on a 1200th anniversary of some kind. The chief thought behind all this, however, was the hope that by doing such a thing they might indirectly impress Stalin.

I had gone to call on my Harvard tutor, Harold J. Laski, in his office at London University to renew old ties, and during my visit I had discussed with him the Moscow proposal. I asked him if he thought a delegation of Anglican Bishops calling on the Russian Orthodox Bishops would indirectly impress Mr. Stalin. Mr. Laski replied that he knew Stalin and had himself just returned from a trip to Moscow. He felt that Mr. Stalin would not be impressed in the slightest by such a move. "But you suggest to the Archbishop of Canterbury that a delegation of Anglican Bishops go directly to the Kremlin—if they can get permission to do so—and call on Mr. Stalin."

I said, "But what in the world would they do there?"

Mr. Laski said the Anglican Bishops should tell Mr. Stalin that they were devoted to peace, but if he provoked a renewal of war, the Bishops would feel obliged to urge their people, the world over, to take up arms against him.

"That," said Mr. Laski, "will impress Mr. Stalin."

It must be explained that in July, 1948 international affairs were quite uneasy.

I went right back to Lambeth Palace and perched myself on a chair in his Grace's office. Doctor Fischer came in and with a great, generous hug said, "Hello, what brings you here?" I told him what Mr. Laski had said. Doctor Fischer whistled, thought awhile and said, "I will go see the Archbishop of York, Doctor Garbeth, you go see Bishop Bell of Chichester and Bishop Oldham of Albany—chairman of the committee on 'The Church and the Modern World'. Let's meet back here at four and see what these gentlemen have to say about Laski's suggestion."

I had good luck both with Bishop Bell and Bishop Oldham, who liked the idea. When I came back and saw Doctor Fischer, he reported rather sadly that he had had no luck at all with the Archbishop of York.

"However," he said, "I am going to see Prime Minister Clement Atlee in the morning and discuss this whole idea with him."

We waited patiently. Nothing ever happened except that in a few days the London papers carried stories that the British government was changing its entire approach to Stalin.

The Bishops never went to Moscow to greet anyone. It was decided that the whole idea was too questionable and risky. But at least I had gotten an agreement from Mr. Laski, on my visit with him, to come to a dinner I was giving at the Union Club for fifty American Bishops, and to address these Bishops on any subject he chose. He accepted the invitation and spoke on the political aspirations of the Roman Catholic Church.

Mr. Laski, an English Jew, serving on a public school board in London, had come to grips with the stubborn and ambitious political designs of the Roman Catholic hierarchy. And so he spoke to the American Bishops about these things, and I must say he had them all sitting on the edges of their seats. In those times no one could even remotely dream that a Pope John XXIII would, much later, appear on the ecclesiastical horizon, and greatly change, and widen, the vision of the Roman Church.

All our time was not spent at Lambeth. Very early in our stay in London, Mrs. du Pont suggested we go out to call on a world-famous physician, Sir James Purvis Stuart, who had written to her a few months before she left Wilmington about the heart-breaking loss of his wife, Lady Stuart. I had frequently come across Sir James and his late wife at dinner parties at "Nemours", the Wilmington home of Mrs. du Pont. I recall the first time I met Sir James. He was seated on Mrs. du Pont's right at dinner and I, on her left. I heard the noted physician saying, "Your Grace."

I looked up from my soup and realized that he was addressing me.

"May I tell you a bit of a story?" he asked. I told him to go ahead, "Please do."

Sir James then related a story about an Englishman who was playing a game of golf all by himself, on St. Andrew's golf course in Scotland. On the adjacent fairway a Scottish gentleman was also playing. Sir James said, "The Scot hit his golf ball a terrible wallop, and the ball hit a tree. It sailed in the Englishman's direction, and hit him in the mouth knocking him down. The Scot, seeing what disaster had overcome the Englishman, rushed to his aid. He picked him up and asked, 'Are you hurt?' 'Well, rather. Besides, you have broken my upper denture.' "

The sympathetic Scot insisted on taking the Englishman to his downtown office, where he put him in a chair and went to a nearby cabinet in search of a denture replacement. Having found one that was very good looking, and fitted perfectly, the Scottish gentleman peered anxiously into the face of the Englishman and said, "Now, sir, you have a beautiful denture. Will you forgive me for the terrible thing I did to you?"

The Englishman, according to Sir James, exclaimed, "I feel greatly indebted to such a fine dentist." To this the Scot, with honest frankness, exclaimed, "Hoot mon—I'm no dentist, I'm an undertaker."

We all loved Sir James, and we felt we had to see him in London as soon as possible to express our deep sympathy over the loss of his wife. Arriving at his home on the outskirts of London, we were admitted by a maid, who astounded us by saying that we would find Lady Stuart standing at the head of the stairs, waiting to welcome us. We were almost afraid to go up. What an eerie experience. What was going on?

A most charming Scottish lady met us at the head of the stairs and took us to the bedside of her husband. Since we knew the first Lady Stuart had been dead now some four or five months, we were in a complete daze. No one explained anything to us and we didn't dare to ask any questions.

The next day at Claridge's I had a call from a well-known physician, a Dr. McKinstry, a distant relative, who happened to be Sir James' physician. I appealed to him for the answer to our puzzle.

The doctor laughed about it and said that sometime back he had ordered a night nurse to come on the job and look after Sir James. But the noted Sir James, being a very eminent and proper gentleman, felt that a woman in his room at night might lead to a scandal. Since he knew a lovely Scottish lady, he had proposed marriage to her by mail and she had accepted. Their marriage was performed at Sir James' bedside. Evidently Sir James' priceless sense of humor did not apply to his personal life style.

Chapter 22

The Queen and the Bishop

During the period of the Lambeth conferences, the Queen of England usually manages to hold a great garden party to which all the Anglican Bishops, from the world over—and their wives—are invited. In 1948, the Bishops had not grown blase about such social events. We looked forward to mingling with some 10,000 guests on the grounds of Buckingham Palace and to glimpsing the King and Queen and Royal Family. The Bishops of the Lambeth Conference had already been received at Buckingham Palace, once or twice, in the earlier days of the conference—but to go to the Queen's garden party was the opportunity of a lifetime.

The Duchess of Northumberland, who was also mistress of the Queen's robes, came to call on us at Claridge's to say that during the Queen's garden party we would be extracted from the multitude, and escorted beyond the restraining ropes, across the greensward, to the Royal tea tent. We were to have tea with Their Majesties, members of the Royal Family and their guests.

While I greatly admired and respected the mistress of the robes, I doubted that such an unusual thing would come to pass. However, the next day Colonel Carnegie of Dundee, Scotland, one of the King's honorary bodyguard, came to call. He acquainted us with the details of the tea party.

The day of the garden party was really beautiful. There must have been at least 10,000 people on the grounds. Our party, consisted of Bishop and Mrs. Juhan of Jacksonville, Florida; Bishop and Mrs. Beverley D.

Tucker of Ohio; Mrs. Jessie Ball du Pont, my wife and myself. We stood at the place we were supposed to be. We waited patiently for Colonel Carnegie to come and to escort us across the lawn to the tea tent. We had told no one about this because we were somewhat fearful that for some reason the event wouldn't take place.

We stood at an opening at the head of an aisle. Down this aisle came Queen Mary in all of her stately elegance and grandeur. She passed us, followed by Princess Margaret and the Mountbattens. Then came a short, rather heavy-set gentleman smoking a cigar. This turned out to be Sir Winston Churchill with Lady Churchill. No one said anything about our following the procession. Our hearts began to sink a bit. Now the guests had assembled under the Royal tea tent and here we were, stranded and presumably forgotten in the place we thought we were supposed to be.

At this point, I spied Colonel Carnegie on the lawn about a hundred feet from us. Before anyone could stop me, I was beyond the restraining ropes and heading for the Colonel. Behind me I could hear a gasp of amazement from the American Bishops and their wives, and I am sure they were saying "Who does he think he is?"

Colonel Carnegie was delighted to see me, saying that he had planned to call for us in the next few minutes. We were joined presently by Lord Gowry, and soon we were being escorted beyond the ropes across the green to the tea tent. When our American friends realized what was happening, they broke all protocol, applauding exuberantly, and many of the people slipped out their movie cameras to record the incident.

Once within the tent we were "presented". I said to Queen Elizabeth, the mother of the present Queen, "Your Majesty, my wife is forever bragging because her birthday is on the same date as yours."

The Queen gave Isabelle a brilliant smile as she

said, "Mrs. McKinstry, I am delighted to know that we have the same birthday; and although I am a week or ten days early, may I now wish you a very happy birthday." I was proud of the curtsy my wife returned as she said, "May I wish you the same, Your Majesty."

We were having a great time with all the Royalty, speaking to them and meeting other people. I wandered to one side of the tent and along came King George VI, accompanied by one of his aides. I heard him say, "Let's get on with this darn party—I want to get home sometime."

I then realized that the large tent next to the tea tent was filled with foreign diplomats, who had to be presented to Their Majesties before the Royal party could break-up. So, taking the hint, I quickly whispered to our group we had better get out. We made our adieux and left. Bishop and Mrs. Juhan, without thinking, started to return the way we had come. I spoke-up and said, "We are not going back the short way. Let's take the longest way out, and enjoy this to the last minute."

Anyway, the next day at Lambeth Conference, some of the Bishops who had been noncommunicative in previous weeks were most gracious to the Bishops of Florida, Ohio and Delaware.

We had two other interesting experiences in England in 1948. We spent one weekend at Windsor Castle, at the time Prince Philip was made a Knight of the Garter. The King and Queen were in residence in the castle. It was a truly magnificent event. Churchill looked very dapper in his gorgeous costume, as did the other Knights of the Garter.

At another time we were entertained at "Ditchley", the English home of the famous Lee family. The Virginia "Ditchley" is the home of the Lee family in the United States, a family made notable by such a member as Robert E. Lee.

Our English host at England's "Ditchley", was Sir Ronald Tree, who told us that Churchill had been resting there when the news had come to him during the Second World War that Rudolf Hess had apparently defected from Nazi Germany, and had landed on the estate of the Duke of Hamilton in Scotland. This was an event which greatly embarrassed the Duke at the time—but it was known authoritatively that the Duke had had no previous knowledge of Hess' plans, and was in no way involved.

The Lambeth Conference came to a close, finally, at a great service at Westminster Abbey. I had invited Mr. and Mrs. George Vandegrift of Wilmington to come over from their London hotel on the Sunday morning of the closing service to have breakfast with us at Claridge's, and to accompany Mrs. McKinstry and me by car to the Abbey for this service. My wife and I had gone down to the lobby at Claridge's to meet our guests, but somehow we missed them because of the many little reception rooms near the lobby.

[184]

Mr. Vandegrift, leaving his wife downstairs, had gone up to our suite to try to find us. He was directed back downstairs by Bishop Juhan, who occupied the suite with us. Bishop Juhan was dressed at the moment in collar and tie and was wearing a white coat. Coming downstairs Mr. Vandegrift found us, and we had a good time at breakfast. After breakfast I went out to get the taxi which I had ordered the previous evening. When I went out the front door with my guests, I expected to find a taxicab but instead I found a beautiful Rolls Royce with a chauffeur in livery. My eyes almost fell out of my head. I groaned inwardly as I wondered how much this was going to cost! We entered the Rolls Royce as if this was something we did every day, and with great nonchalance we were driven to the Abbey. We returned by bus.

When I got back to the States, I found that George Vandegrift had written to our Wilmington friends, saying, "Believe it or not, he had a valet who met me at the door of his suite and directed me to the lobby where I found the Bishop. But after breakfast the Bishop and his wife put us in their Rolls Royce which was driven by a chauffeur in livery, and we went to the Abbey in style. My gracious! What a man!"

Another memorable experience at Lambeth was meeting the Right Reverend Andrew Y. Y. Tsu, Bishop of the Burma Road in China. He impressed me in many ways. When I returned to Delaware I invited him to come to the diocese to visit our parishes, to preach and to confirm. Bishop Tsu had been expelled from China by the Communists. He is now (1975) living at the Methodist Country House, and has been revisiting parishes in the absence of a Bishop in this diocese (because of the unfortunate death of Bishop William H. Mead) and I am told that the people are overjoyed to see him and to hear him again.

[185]

Following our exciting time in England and Scotland, we took the boat for Paris and the Continent.

In Rome we stayed at the Excelsior Hotel at the same time the Shah of Iran and his first wife were registered there. We had seen them at Claridge's earlier in the summer. The Roman opera authorities had decided to stage a gala performance of "Aida" in honor of the Shah and his wife. Our party decided to take advantage of this unusual opportunity. We drove to the opera house in a rented limousine. When the crowds which had gathered to see the Shah saw our party go by, they looked at me—a rather short and dark little fellow and began to shout, "There he goes, there he goes." This produced a big laugh in the car.

"Aida" was staged in the ruins of the baths of Caracalla, under a full Italian moon—we were emotionally drained by the end of the performance.

Before our stay in Rome was over, we had the rare privilege of being entertained by Dr. and Mrs. Ruggieri of Rome. Dr. Ruggieri was a banker. My wife, always a beautiful dancer, had a wonderful time on the dance floor with her host, who danced very well, too. I talked with the banker's wife at the table and, between dances, with her husband. They gave me some very interesting sidelights concerning the status of the Roman Catholic Church in Italy in 1948.

Dr. Ruggieri said they and many of their friends liked Pope Pius very much. "He is a nice man and we would love to see him more often." Then he went on to say that they cordially disliked the hierarchy surrounding the Pope. They complained to us that many of these officials of the church lived like princes during the Second World War.

I asked them if they ever went to religious services. They admitted they did not, except at Easter time to see the Easter pageantry. Mrs. Ruggieri said that sometimes she went into churches by herself in the daytime simply to sit there and to think and meditate, but never to church services.

I stammered out a surprise comment. I had always assumed that it was the Roman Catholic Church which had saved Italy from becoming Communist after the Second World War. They both laughed at this. The banker said, "It was the Marshall Plan that saved Italy—nothing else."

The banker's wife complained that the Roman Catholic hierarchy ignored the poor, in her opinion, and yet the church lived on the support and loyalty of the poor. I was quite shocked by his frank discussion on the part of our hosts, who were responsible Roman citizens of affluence and social prominence. I asked them if they had many friends who felt the same way. They said they did, but they probably wouldn't tell us as frankly, how they felt.

Finally, Dr. Ruggieri said very solemnly, "The Roman Church will not be a helpful, constructive influence in Rome or in Italy until there is a rebirth of the spirit of St. Francis of Assisi."

It is nothing short of a miracle that the world later witnessed that rebirth of St. Francis' spirit in the life and ministry of Pope John XXIII, who came on the scene many years later. John had been expected to be merely a "caretaker" pope, but he surprised the entire church and was, in truth, the founder of a new, fresh era in Roman Catholicism, and indeed in the whole world. It was the work of God. Is it too much to hope that the Roman Catholic Church may be able to live up to the vision that Pope John XXIII had regarding his beloved church?

After a final week in Paris at the Ritz, we returned to London. Mrs. McKinstry and I took leave of our friends and got aboard the old Queen Elizabeth bound for New York.

Chapter 23

My Father and
President Truman

I give full credit to my father, Leslie I. McKinstry, for my religious upbringing, and for developing my interest in all religions. When he heard from my own lips at the age of ten that I intended to prepare for the ministry, he systematically took me to all types of churches in my home town in Kansas.

He was on very friendly terms with the local Roman Catholic rector, and I was taken every two or three months to Mass in the Roman Church. After several years of this, I became familiar with their services and also attended occasionally the Service of Benediction, which I really never liked.

He encouraged me to join the Christian Endeavor Society, which was then in operation in the Presbyterian Church. I also became a member of the youth group in the Methodist Church. In my own Episcopal Church I was present each Sunday morning for the eight o'clock Communion Service, and I usually served at the altar. I was a member of the Sunday School and I attended morning prayer at eleven o'clock in my parish church.

My parents had been Episcopalians since their early married life when they forsook the Methodist Church to be confirmed according to Anglican tradition. They had a general appreciation of all the churches and I inherited their interest and concern. I sincerely believe that living in a small town, and being a member of a small Episcopal congregation—with intimate contact with all the churches—rather conditioned me for a ministry in a small, compact almost rural diocese like Delaware.

More about my father: he used to visit Bishopstead during the Christmas season each year, arriving perhaps a month before that festal season, and I used to put him to work. It was my custom to call on each rector in the diocese on the two days prior to Christmas and to leave presents for the rectors, their wives and children. My wife, Isabelle, helped me by buying the presents throughout the year. When my father came, she induced him to wrap these many packages.

On the numerous journeys to Wilmington, between Thanksgiving and Christmas, my father would hint that sometime we should go to Washington and call on President and Mrs. Harry S. Truman at the White House. I have mentioned earlier in this record that the McKinstrys had once lived in Independence, Missouri, where my father was the organist and choirmaster at Trinity Episcopal Church. In that capacity, he had known Bess Wallace, later Mrs. Truman, and he had also known the Trumans. They were not Episcopalians. Father had taught Bess Wallace in Sunday School and trained her in the junior choir. Therefore, it was logical he should flirt with the idea of calling on the Trumans at the White House. He delayed the visit, saying, "Let's see whether the President makes good."

[189]

On his last visit to Bishopstead, I reminded my father the Trumans were leaving the White House early in the following year and I suggested that he not wait any longer. He agreed. So, we made arrangements to go to Washington. We took with us Governor Elbert N. Carvel and his father. Our meeting with the President was extraordinary.

The President was in great form. He seemed to be addressing himself to me, for I sat directly across the desk from him. He made a mystifying statement: "Bishop, I am the most powerful man who has ever lived since the beginning of civilization. More so than Alexander the Great, Julius Caesar, Ghengis Khan or Napoleon Bonaparte—they weren't in it with me. Every time I speak, I affect the lives of millions upon millions of people all over this world."

I made no comment. He continued, "Of course, it means long hours for me. I can't do many of the things I would like to do."

My father, a sensitive gentleman, never forgave me for my rejoinder: "Mr. President, in view of all you say about your position in world history—and your long and arduous hours—it does seem to me, sir, that after seven years of the Presidency you look remarkably hale and hearty."

The President didn't blink. He replied, "It is my system. Why, during the terms of Teddy Roosevelt, Taft, Wilson, Hoover and even FDR, this office was chaotic. It remained for me to systematize it.

"Every morning, precisely at ten o'clock, I press that button and my executive assistants come in to confer with me. So, every morning I know everything going on all over the world."

I think the President himself became a little tired of this conversation because he suggested we leave that particular area of the office and go across the room to inspect a global map. He said, "Get down on your knees, Bishop—you are used to doing such things—and read what you see on that silver plate there."

On my knees I read the engraved plate: "Presented to President Harry S. Truman by General of the Army Dwight D. Eisenhower."

The President said, "Now turn the globe around and read what is on that other plate."

I obediently followed his instructions and read, "Returned to President-Elect Dwight D. Eisenhower by President Harry S. Truman."

Former Governor Elbert N. Carvel

Houston Wilson, Esq.

The President smiled his pleasure as he said, "Isn't that nice?"

It was hard for me to believe that on that very day the President had said perfectly terrible things about President-Elect Eisenhower in the newspapers. I suspect it was because the President wanted Mr. Eisenhower to run on the Democratic ticket. Anyhow, such is politics.

When we took our leave of the White House, Governor Carvel, his father, my father and I went to the Washington Cathedral and arrived on time for Evensong. In the vast chancel of the church we participated in a beautiful service. The famed Boys Choir came marching in, following a crucifer. I must say when the boys saw Governor Carvel (some six feet six or seven inches tall) they almost forgot what they were there for. And when they heard his booming voice singing all of the hymns with great heartiness, they almost missed their cues.

[192] I am very happy my father was able to visit the Trumans because it was his last Christmas at Bishopstead. On his way home to Denver he died on the train.

Chapter 24

A Coadjutor

Our trip abroad in 1948 had convinced me that my wife and I should travel more. We knew we could never travel quite so luxuriously as we had then, but we should travel nonetheless. I felt that as long as we owned our summer home in Massachusetts— "Meadowmere", a 1710 house situated in the lovely country between Ipswich and Newburyport—we would feel obliged to return to it. We had always loved this Massachusetts home, which we had acquired in 1927, because our four children had practically grown up there. It was a beautiful, safe, handy countryside, five hours from Albany when we lived there and about twelve hours from Wilmington, before the building of the expressways.

In 1947, we decided to sell "Meadowmere". We had had a difficult time during the Second World War, when no help was available in the country, and when small privileges, such as use of the laundry in Newburyport were denied us because we were "summer people". We were kept going, thank goodness, by a friendly farmer, who raised delicious garden stuff and provided us with chickens, eggs and milk. So I listed the place with an Ipswich real estate agent, who gleefully said he could sell it very promptly. However, a prospective purchaser had made some rather indiscreet remarks about some of our neighbors, and my wife, vastly irritated, asked me to write to the agent, withdrawing the house from the market.

This I did. But the agent tried to sell the place

just the same, and eventually wired that he had sold it to a Navy officer. He asked us to confirm the sale. Since I was unavailable, my wife wired back a refusal to confirm, stating that her children had unexpectedly objected to the sale. At that point, the greedy real estate agent sued us for the full commission. Later, the basis of the suit was changed to that of a demand that we give title to the property to the intended purchaser.

Finally, we went to court to settle the matter; and, since I was ill in the hospital, in Wilmington, I sent word to my lawyer in Boston that I had decided to raise the price of the property. If the Navy officer, who desired to buy it so badly, would pay the increased price, I would settle out of court—otherwise they could sue until the cows came home! The Navy officer decided to accept my offer, and everything was settled. So ended our New England vacations.

About this time, I became convinced that Mrs. McKinstry, who seemed tired, should go to Cleveland Clinic for a checkup. I wanted very much to go myself but I told her I didn't dare announce to the public that I was going to the clinic because people would talk too much. But if she would go to Cleveland and make it clear that she was really the patient, I could hide behind her skirts. She agreed to this.

After two days of examinations, my wife was pronounced in reasonably good shape, but I had gall stones! With considerable apprehension, I asked if an operation was called for, but the clinic informed me that they thought not—at least at that time.

Returning to Wilmington, I confided in my physician at the University of Pennsylvania Hospital. He asked me to visit the hospital at once and to discuss the whole matter with him and the noted surgeon, Dr. Ravdin. The latter practically ordered me to go into the operating room, but I resisted and said I would wait until I had some pain, or more discomfort.

This I never did have. However, a year or two later I developed diabetes. This was a considerable shock to me. So the accumulation of ailments, beginning with a heart failure in 1942—which almost finished me—and acute infectious jaundice in 1947, followed by discovery of gall stones and the diabetes in 1950 and 1951, took its toll.

I knew that I was beginning to slip physically, since I could not carry-out my work with vigor. My faithful secretary, Miss Emily D. Goode, who, with me, comprised the diocesan office force, stood up marvelously well under occasionally questionable treatment because of my tensions, frustrations and physical limitations. I had indeed burned the candle at both ends through the years.

The Reverend Doctor William C. Munds, rector of Christ Church Christiana Hundred, asked me to meet with him, and some of his friends, to talk about my health. They told me that certain laymen in the diocese had provided for the private financing of a Bishop Coadjutor if I would agree to accept one. The idea was to keep me active as the diocesan Bishop as long as possible. At first I demurred, but after considerable persuasion I finally accepted the generous offer.

I notified the standing committee of the diocese. I obtained permission from the House of Bishops for the election of a Coadjutor and asked, of course, the permission of the diocesan convention. They all gave approval at once, with the understanding that the diocese would not be responsible for the salary of the Coadjutor. I appointed a special committee, men of excellence and wisdom, to look for suitable nominees for the new post. Naturally, the Coadjutor would succeed to the office of diocesan upon my retirement.

There is a difference between a Bishop Coadjutor and a Suffragan Bishop. The latter serves without right of succession. The old cliche' says that when the Suffragan comes into the office of the Bishop in the morning, bright-eyed and eager, he asks the Bishop what he can do to help him that day.

But it is alleged that when the Coadjutor comes in, he looks the Bishop over very carefully and after some scrutiny, asks rather cautiously the question, "How do you feel?"

Well, the special committee searched far and wide. They wrote many letters to many dioceses and to a great many Bishops. Finally they decided they were ready to report. They asked me to come to a meeting of the committee so I might hear what they had to say. The meeting took place in the parish house of Christ Church Christiana Hundred.

The committee reported that it had been told by distinguished churchmen, including the many Bishops to whom they had written, that Delaware had among its clergy potential Bishops as good as could be found anywhere outside the state. They had therefore decided thay they would nominate three clergy in Delaware; namely, the Reverend Paul A. Kellogg of Christ Church, Dover; the Reverend William H. Marmion of St. Andrew's Church, Wilmington; and the Very Reverend J. Brooke Mosley, Dean of St. John's Cathedral, Wilmington. They stated it would be understood, of course, that other nominations could be made from the floor at the time of the convention called to elect. A full report then was sent by the committee to all the clergy of the diocese and to the delegates to the forthcoming special convention.

[196]

The convention assembled in Immanuel Church, Wilmington. A few nominations were made from the floor. However, after many, many ballots, the delegates chose Dean Mosley as the Bishop Coadjutor. He was approved by the House of Bishops, and by a majority of the standing committees of the whole church. Dean Mosley was consecrated Bishop Coadjutor in the Cathedral Church of St. John on October 28, 1953.

Unfortunately, my health did not improve even with this additional help granted me. In fact, it got worse. In late November 1954, my doctors at the University of Pennsylvania Hospital and at Bryn Mawr had a consulation and ordered me to resign forthwith—effective December 31, 1954—"either this, or risk disaster".

A wonderful church service was held in the Cathedral in December of 1954, commemorating officially the close of another chapter in the history of the Diocese of Delaware; and there was a very fine reception given to Mrs. McKinstry and me, and our family, at the Hotel Du Pont. Throughout it all, great dignity and good taste was in evidence. I was grateful to God for having had the high privilege of serving for so many years as Diocesan in a wonderful diocese full of warm and responsive friends.

Chapter 25

Retirement

The retirement days were upon us.

Nothing is more dramatic in human life than facing retirement; especially is this true of a person who has led a very active life and held important public positions. For a man in good health, retirement can be an ordeal. However, for a person who is ill and has been forced to retire early, retirement can be something of a nightmare.

Ideally, a person about to retire does well to plan on staying in the community where he has lived and worked, and where he has friends. Readjustment is thus very much easier. Contrariwise, when a person gives up his occupation and goes to a completely strange community, making friends late in life is not always an easy thing to do.

However, I had always placed great stress on the importance of a clergyman's departure from the scene of his labors—to avoid getting into his successor's hair, so to speak. Thus, I felt that, having preached this sort of thing all my life, especially after I became Bishop, in my own retirement I must practice what I had preached. I felt I must not only leave the place of my previous residence, but I must move from my beloved Delaware. There could not be any evasion of this proper procedure. So the main question was, where would Mrs. McKinstry and I live?

We had had a truly wonderful life in San Antonio from 1931 through August 1938, and we had hundreds of dear friends there. I rather hesitatingly suggested to my dear wife that San Antonio might be a place to which we could go for our retirement years. But I knew in my own heart, even before I'd made the suggestion, that in spite of her love for San Antonio, this would not be acceptable; she was a mother, and a mother wants to be near her children and grandchildren. The same conclusion was forthcoming when I rather timidly mentioned Sewanee, Tennessee.

Of course, we could not know definitely where our children would be living through the remainder of our years. Our oldest daughter, Isabelle, married to Paul Stadler, a Navy officer, would be likely to move about as she and her husband had done for years. I think they must have lived in seventeen or eighteen places since they have been married. However, we felt that when Paul ultimately retired from active service (he probably would do so earlier than most men because of the length of his service) he and his family would live in the east.

We felt the same would be true of the other [199] children: Margaret (Maull), Barbara (Lawton), James Thomas, the lawyer and our youngest, Arthur St. Clair, who as yet had not decided on a career. Therefore, we felt rather compelled to find a place somewhere in the east.

During the early 1950's, I had visited Easton, Maryland, several times, the first at the time of the meeting of our Third Provincial Synod. On our visits, we had been greatly impressed by the beauty of Talbot County and the neatness of Easton, an old colonial town. Mr. Johnson Grimes had returned there upon retirement and had built Tidewater Inn, a most charming example of colonial architecture, and it seemed to us that this Inn had added greatly to the desirability of the area. Much of the public social life of Talbot County and the Eastern Shore was centered at the Inn. Besides, it seemed to us that the Inn would be an ideal place, not only for us to meet the local residents, but also for entertainment of out-of-town guests. So, little by little, we began to consider Easton as a good site for our retirement home. It was, after all, within two hours of Wilmington, if we felt the urge to visit our former home occasionally; surely we would still go to our doctors there and in nearby Pennsylvania. Then, too, Philadelphia and New York were not too far away, and Baltimore and Washington were relatively nearby. Altogether, Easton seemed to us an ideal location for our purposes.

While an officer of our National Council in New York, I had met Francis Bartlett, a real estate agent in Easton and the son-in-law of the late Bishop John Gardner Murray of the Diocese of Maryland. I called on the Bartlett firm and asked them to help us look for a waterfront home somewhere near Easton.

My wife and I had always loved the water. She was reared in Cleveland, and her family's summer home on Lake Erie was a beautiful place at the confluence of Rocky River and the lake, opposite the Cleveland Yacht Club. While living in Cleveland as rector of the Church of the Incarnation, I had become a boat enthusiast. My wife's father and brother were avid yachtsmen.

So we specified to Mr. Bartlett that our retirement home must be within sight of Talbot County's beautiful waters. I was informed the county has some 600 or more miles of shore line.

Our attention was soon directed to a portion of an extensive estate, the old Tweedy farm, located on Peach Blossom stream, five miles from Easton, on the Oxford Road. The portion of the farm in which we became interested consisted of an interesting house and three or four acres on which were more than a hundred trees. And it was in full open view of the wide Peach Blossom. Indeed, we could look downstream from our lawn and see where the Peach Blossom is joined by the Tred Avon in its sweep towards Oxford.

A few hundred feet to the left of the house, and facing the stream, was the manor house. It was in the center of a plot of twelve acres, with gorgeous trees and shrubs. "Oaklands" was the name of the Tweedy farm, and the house we became interested in bore the name of "Oaklands Cottage". It was a bright yellow, two-story frame house which had been added to from time to time.

The house had an enormous screened front porch, and there was an upstairs gallery of the same size. Immediately adjacent to the porch was a huge living room, thirty-six feet by twenty feet, with a fifteen foot ceiling. At the end of this room was a large fireplace.

There were no other residences on the Tweedy farm at that time other than the large brick manor house and Oaklands Cottage which we were considering. Thus we were assured of complete privacy.

One of the choice assets of the property was a wonderful water well, at least 500 feet deep, which had an ample supply of soft and palatable water. It originated in a stream which had cleared the mountains of western Maryland, and had swept to us from under the Chesapeake Bay. This well had served as the sole source of water for the owners in their respective homes, and for the farm cottages. We decided to take Oaklands Cottage, and agreed to receive title in the spring of 1955.

Meanwhile, there was the cruel and unnerving task of cleaning out our belongings at Bishopstead. This we grimly accomplished by might and main. We put our goods in storage the first week in January, 1955, and shortly after left Delaware by motorcar for San Antonio for an extended rest. In that hospitable city, our close friends received us warmly and, for the time being made us forget the sorrow of leaving Delaware.

After a very pleasant stay, which included a tour of Mexico, we returned to Easton late in April, took title to our new home, and shortly thereafter moved-in. We were aided in this ordeal by the late Walter Johnson, one of Philadelphia's most respected interior decorators. It was Mr. Johnson who greased the wheels of the moving operation, and who showed us how to make our new home attractive.

When I told the Bartlett real estate firm of our need for two able men to wash windows, clean the house and spruce up the grounds, they sent two excellent men. One, Chester Andrews, a huge fellow with a great, deep voice, told me that his wife, Mildred, was at the moment available in case we needed a maid. We engaged her at once. She was with us all through our stay at Oaklands Cottage, and she turned out to be one of the finest maids, and one of the best friends we ever had. She was a wonderful person and a great cook.

When we had party or a family get-together, her husband also helped. He had formerly been a butler, but preferred to do outside work. He looked after our grounds all the time we lived in Talbot County. Our children affectionately called Mildred, "Mo", and they were also very keen about her husband, Chester.

I had come down to Easton very discouraged about myself and my immediate future and, I am almost ashamed to say, ready to "cash in my chips". But inheriting Mildred and Chester boosted my morale. They were an unusual couple and they made us happy.

This is a little out of context, but when Mildred died after we had come back to Wilmington in 1964, Mrs. McKinstry and I went to the funeral. As we sat in the Negro church, which was packed to the doors, the pastor came to me to ask me to follow him. I went to the head of the church nave, up the steps to the platform and was introduced to two or three other clergymen. I was then asked to preach the sermon at the service, and to officiate at the grave in the nearby cemetery. I considered this a very great honor indeed—and it was a most moving experience for me and my wife.

Naturally, we began to attend religious services at Christ Episcopal Church in Easton. A few people spoke to us in the beginning—more later on—and soon we felt relatively at ease and at home there. The Bishop of Easton, the Right Reverend Allen J. Miller, and his wife came to call on us at Oaklands Cottage, and they gave a dinner for us at the Tidewater Inn as a welcome to Easton.

Because I had been a Rotarian since 1927, when I first went to Albany, I felt at liberty to attend the Wednesday luncheons of the Easton Rotary Club, there I met some fine, friendly men.

Even with these advantages, it seemed very strange, at first, to walk the streets of Easton and see so few people we knew. During my years in Wilmington, I never dared take my eyes off the face of an approaching person on the street lest I miss a friend, or someone who at least knew me and wished to speak. Mrs. McKinstry, who frequented the downtown Wilmington stores, had loads of friends who always greeted her.

This awareness of a feeling of "not yet belonging", was a part of the agony of readjustment. However, conditions gradually improved. Yet it was not to be expected that a "foreign" retired Bishop would receive the recognition he had known in his former diocese.

My family surprised me by providing a twenty foot boat with an outboard motor. A local hardware proprietor had his men build a fifty foot dock for me to accommodate the new boat. We christened it "The Happy Mac". As soon as I learned how to operate the boat, it became a source of great pleasure. All of my children, and their offspring, loved to take trips on the various streams of Talbot County. Many of these streams were famous because of the handsome residences along the banks.

Some of our guests also enjoyed boating. Once my son Arthur and I took Mr. and Mrs. Harold W. Horsey of Dover on a ride downstream to Oxford. On the return trip we ran out of gas about a half-mile from home. We poled the boat to the dock of a friend, a Mr. White, who was a famous Princeton football player in his day.

My son was embarrassed about this because it was his responsibility to see that there was sufficient gasoline on board. He borrowed Mr. White's car and went off for a can of gasoline. Eventually we were on our way to home port.

The greatest single bit of morale building, for me personally, was a famous law suit. It completely diverted me from my ills. It happened in this manner: two prominent men in Easton had purchased the remainder of the Tweedy farm. The land was classified as "waterfront" property, according to the Talbot zoning laws. These men decided to try for a zoning change. Contiguous to our property there stretched a quarter of a mile of land which was not actually on the water, although classified as waterfront property. The new owners felt that if the restrictions, requiring at least two acres for waterfront classification, were lifted they could divide the land into sixty foot lots and make a fortune.

Inasmuch as there was no sewerage system available to prospective buyers of these lots, each owner would have to install his own cesspool and drill his own well. From the public health angle alone this was a rather frightening idea. The houses erected on sixty foot lots would not be very substantial and, therefore, they would be a threat to other property values in the area.

I repeatedly consulted public health authorities about this, and they told me the end result would probably be bad. I began to drop in on nearby neighbors to discuss our common danger. They threw up their hands in despair, but gave as their opinion that no one could successfully resist such well-to-do men. I disagreed with this point of view and proceeded to enlist all the help I could find.

We had a series of home meetings, to which a growing number of property owners came, including, for example, Mrs. Alton B. Jones, the wife of the then president of the Cities Service Oil Company. Gradually our community engine began to pick up steam.

We engaged an ambitious young lawyer to represent our group, which now numbered close to a hundred people. He worked very hard and concluded we should take the issue to court. Judge Dewees Carter, was the presiding judge. Our experts took the stand as well as certain waterfront property owners. We had one or two real estate agents who had the courage to bear testimony against the proposal. But most of the Easton agents fled, when invited to give their opinions in court. They feared the wrath of power.

The two lawyers who represented the zoning board, and the men who sought to have the zoning laws changed, did their best. But our lawyer did better. The court decided in our favor, and the Talbot zoning laws remained "as is". Pandemonium broke out, anger was expressed. The businessmen, who had never before had an experience of this nature, decided to appeal Judge Carter's decision. They took the case to the Maryland Supreme Court.

Some time elapsed before the decision came down. During this time I often received a cold, unfriendly [205] stare from our adversaries when I met them on the street. One evening at the Talbot County Country Club, one of the opposing lawyers came-over to me and said, "Bishop, the Supereme Court has upheld Judge Carter's ruling. We tried our best to lick you, but we failed. Now that it's all over, permit me, as a citizen of Talbot County, to thank you and your group for having saved Talbot County."

This took considerable courage. It was the action of a real Christian gentlemen.

The waterfront property owners, of course in the county rejoiced. It is not an overstatement to say that our victory had an inestimable effect on land values in Talbot County. The disappointed owners were pretty much disgusted, but they had other plans.

One immediate reaction was the announcement that they intended to bulldoze trees and shrubs on a beautiful four-and-a-half acre plot immediately beyond the manor house. They planned to use this valuable area as an approach to a large public dock which they would build, presumably as a gimmick for selling the land behind Oaklands Cottage, and the rest of the peninsula to the right of us. This threat caused us deep concern. A public dock operated without strict rules and supervision could be a big nuisance, and it could not help but devalue nearby estates. What could we do to stop this act, which seemed pretty much one of vengeance?

I went to Washington to consult the congressman from the Eastern Shore and others in Congress. I was told I could not stop the proposed public dock through any action on their part. It was suggested that I see the United States Army Engineers in Baltimore. This was done. We received no help from them either, because government engineers never mix in local politics.

Returning to Easton I called on my young neighbor, Joseph Whitehill, and proposed that he and I secretly buy the four-and-a-half acres and do it at once. Mr. Whitehill was agreeable. He engaged the assistance of a Washington banker, a close friend of his father, who in turn was a well-known oil man in Oklahoma. We asked the banker to buy the acreage for us and to pay anything necessary to get it. He was expert in the handling of the deal. The amount offered the owners was too large to turn down. They consoled one another by deciding to place the public dock at some other location.

So Mr. Whitehill and I wound up with a beautiful building site, probably the most desirable left in Talbot County, at a price higher than ever had been paid before for one of such dimensions.

It was quite amusing to visit many friends and neighbors, and listen to their explosive remarks about the idiots who had reputedly paid "too much" for the acreage involved. Later, when the property was registered there were many red faces in the community. It soon became apparent, however, that we had done our neighbors a good turn by saving property values.

The "dock builders" were infuriated when they found they had been defeated a second time. But, I was still uneasy. The promise made in the presence of the banker to locate the public dock elsewhere bothered me no end. I recalled that on the right of Oaklands Cottage, these men owned a narrow outlet to the water, about thirty feet in width, which connected with their land. This would make a perfect location for the public dock, and it would be close to the area they had planned a subdivision of sixty foot lots.

Such a move would be more disastrous than the first plan, which Mr. Whitehill and I had spent good money to defeat. As I had been the spear-head of the property owner movement I felt compelled to act quickly. I wrote to the United States Army Engineers in Baltimore and frankly confessed that I had been living in sin. I told them that when I came to Easton I was ignorant of water rights, so, I hired a man to build a fifty foot dock. Needless to say, I assumed the man knew of any restrictions. Continuing in my letter, I wrote that I had no idea at the time that it was essential for one to get permission from the government for a dock like mine. I apologized for my ignorance, and asked them to forgive me.

Then I went on to explain that the water at my dock was very shallow, and guests coming to call on me in larger boats were unable to dock. They had to anchor some distance off shore and come to my dock in a rowboat. I ended by asking the engineers for permission to extend my dock another one hundred feet, with a thirty-five foot ell to the right, behind which I would moor my own boat. To my great surprise, permission was granted. Almost instantly I had the materials to do the job and the work was completed within a week's time.

We waited for what possibly might happen—some sort of repercussion. Sure enough, one day a boat came down the Peach Blossom with two men aboard. One was a noted dock-builder, and the other one of our public dock opponents. They stopped the boat some distance away, stood-up and viewed my new dock with surprise. They apparently had not heard of this development. My dock extension, and the ell, had cut off any opportunity left for them to build a public dock.

I learned later that they tried to persuade the Army engineers to amputate my dock, but this they refused to do. So ended another attempt to build a nuisance.

Naturally, I was now quite unpopular with those ambitious men. No one was quite sure, during all the maneuvering, just what my motives were—but, there was no public dock. Ultimately, one was built at Legates Cove, on the other side of the peninsula. All this excitement was enjoyed by this neophyte waterman, and it caused me to forget all about my personal ills.

Perhaps the two men, to whom I have referred, admired my resistance and resourcefulness, for one of them, after several years, began to speak to me on the street. His brother, however, never could "see me". Too bad, because I liked him.

Chapter 26

Travel

During the remainder of our stay in Talbot County, we had no more issues over which to fight. Life became serene and pleasant. We often entertained our friends, many coming down from Wilmington. Our children and grandchildren loved to visit, especially on holidays during the summer. Naturally my health improved, although the diabetes was destined to be a permanent difficulty.

Early in my residence in Talbot County, I had proof that our decision to move away from Wilmington had been a wise one. One day the senior warden of one of Wilmington's important parishes telephoned me that he was coming to see me the next night, bringing his entire vestry with him. The purpose was a need to confer about their problems. I replied that if they came, I would not let them in.

"Besides," I said, "you have a Bishop. Go see him."

It is my feeling that had I stayed on in Wilmington, that particular group, and possibly others, might have come to call without warning. There was no need of this because they had plenty of advice at hand without bothering me. My safe distance from Delaware precluded such incidents.

However, I had ample opportunity to do a little work for the Bishop of Easton behind the scenes. Bishop Miller always received me very cordially whenever I went to call on him in his downtown office. But it always seemed to me that he looked quite worried and often gray and drawn. I felt he was carrying a great load and that this would ultimately impair his health unless his burden was lightened. I asked him one day what was on his mind, and he confessed he had little or no money with which to take advantage of opportunities for growth and development in the diocese.

Before very long, I happened to attend the eightieth birthday party of the late Mrs. Francis I. du Pont, given by her children in Wilmington. Among the guests was the late Donaldson Brown, a very important and well-to-do person from the Eastern Shore. I took Mr. Brown into a small side room, where I talked to him very frankly about his Bishop and his diocese. I told him how the Bishop had no funds to work with, and I thought it was a great source of anxiety to him . . . I didn't see why the people of Easton didn't channel some of their resources through the Bishop's discretionary fund.

I explained that many people in Wilmington had been doing this for the Diocese of Delaware for years. Mr. Brown was apparently impressed because he asked me, when I returned to Easton, to make an engagement to lunch with a Mr. Kellogg, of Old Wye Church, and tell him my story.

I did this, and Mr. Kellogg agreed that year-end funds should, and could, be channelled by people of means to the Bishop's discretionary fund. He said he would get in touch with Mr. Brown. Weeks later when I called on Bishop Miller near the end of the year, he was radiantly happy as he exhibited a check in five figures from Donaldson Brown. I never told him what I had done. Mr. Brown continued to send a substantial check each year-end, until his death. His will also generously remembered diocesan endowment funds.

At the end of 1965, after I had moved back to Wilmington, Bishop Miller realized that for health reasons he would have to retire from the active ministry. I persuaded a few loyal churchmen in the Diocese of Easton to join with me, and some of the more generous churchmen in Wilmington, in raising funds for a retirement home for Bishop and Mrs. Miller in Naples, Florida, where they desired to go.

We were able to raise $30,000. At my suggestion, the Bishop deeded his property immediately to the Diocese of Easton. When it is no longer used by the Millers, the diocese will receive the proceeds of the sale of the Naples property. The money will be set-up as an endowment fund for the diocese. Bishop and Mrs. Miller have entertained me in their new home in Naples, and they are exceedingly proud of it, and, I might add, they deserved it.

In 1958, we had some very exciting times abroad. Late in 1957 we received a most gracious letter from a generous Wilmington gentleman and churchman, an old friend, William Winder (Chick) Laird, telling us he and his wife loved to travel abroad and they suspected that we, too, liked to travel. This extraordinary person said, "We want you to go to Europe this summer at our expense." There was wild excitement at Oaklands Cottage the day that letter arrived.

[211]

We were told there would be a car and chauffeur in Britain, and one on the Continent at our disposal. Of course, we accepted this most generous offer with great appreciation.

After the routine of securing reservations on ships and at numerous hotels abroad, we sailed on June 20, 1958 for Southhampton and London. This time there would be no Claridge's Hotel for us, but rather a nice and modest hostel by the name of St. Ermin's, not far from Westminster Abbey. We found other Bishops there who had come to attend the 1958 Lambeth Conference which would be opening in a few days at Canterbury Cathedral. For example: Bishop and Mrs. Gerald F. Burrill of Chicago; Bishop and Mrs. Charles C. J. Carpenter of Alabama; Bishop and Mrs. Edward Hamilton West of Florida and Bishop Horace W. B. Donegan of New York were registered there.

The day we arrived in London, we discovered that Mrs. Ellason Downs of Wilmington was staying at Hotel Connaught. When she heard from us, she insisted we have lunch with her in that fine hotel the next day. She gave us the tragic news that Miss Lydia du Pont, daughter of the late A. Felix du Pont, had been killed in an automobile accident. This was indeed shocking news. It was only ten years earlier, that we learned of her father's sudden death, while we were at the 1948 Lambeth Conference.

On Wednesday, July 2, 1958, after checking out of our hotel, our chauffeur called for us and our tour of England and Scotland began. We first stopped at Rochester Cathedral to see its fine architecture and famous glass. We arrived at Canterbury that night and put up at the local Inn. Shortly after we arrived, we visited St. Martin's Church, a twelfth century edifice, one of England's oldest.

On Thursday, July 3, we attended the great opening service of Lambeth Conference at Canterbury. This time I sat in the nave. In 1948, I had been in the sanctuary not far from the Archbishop of Canterbury. Later that day, I conferred with the Reverend David Rose who had, at my suggestion, served as rector of the Church of the Good Shepherd, Corpus Christi, Texas, but, who now had been elected the Suffragan Bishop of Southern Virginia. At the end of our conference, I strongly advised him to accept his election. Today, he is the Bishop of Southern Virginia.

On July 4, my wife and I continued our tour of England. We visited the Town of Witney, the seat of the important woolen business. Mrs. McKinstry was especially interested in this place, where her English family is still producing wool and making the famous Early (Witney) blankets. The company has been in existence for over 300 years.

We had phoned ahead to inform Patrick Early, the president of the company, that we were going to call on him. When we arrived at the factory Mr. Early had his oldest employee all dressed up and waiting to greet us. This gracious man informed us a board of directors meeting was in progress and that until it was concluded we were to be entertained by the president's mother and father. When the elderly Mrs. Early heard that we had arrived, she came dashing through the garden gate, embraced my wife and warmly welcomed us. She conducted us through the beautiful garden to the ancient house, where we met her husband.

My wife was especially delighted to be in the house where her great-great-grandfather Early had lived when he was the president of the Early Blanket Company. On the walls were family portraits and pictures of English royalty. When the meeting of the board was over, we went back to the main offices, where Patrick Early served us high tea.

The next day we went to Coughton Court, a magnificent Fourteenth century country house, now a national trust house and museum. There we saw for the first time the famous Coxeter Coat and took pictures of it in its glass case. Coxeter was my wife's ancestor, who married into the Early family.

It seems that young Coxeter, in times when there were no great national pastimes or games, and certainly no TV or radio, decided to enliven life a little by making a bet. He wagered that between sunup and sundown on a given day, he would be able to shear the sheep, process the wool, weave and dye the cloth and, with the help of a local tailor, have a handsome frock coat on the back of Lord Throckmorton. The wager had been made well in advance of the deed, and people everywhere in England who heard of it were greatly excited about this brash claim. Young Coxeter won his bet. Tradition has it that even the king summoned him to bring the coat to him so that he might see it. The coat has, therefore, been a famous item and has been well preserved through the years in its protective case.

Driving up to the English lake country, which we saw for the first time (always that countryside reminds me of the country on either side of Montchanin Road, Wilmington, going from Pennsylvania Avenue over to Route 202), we finally reached Scotland and the seat of one of my Scottish family places, Rosslyn, a little south of Edinburgh. We loved seeing the beautiful Rosslyn Chapel and, of course, the remnants of the castle, the latter having been largely destroyed by Cromwell. I mentioned the chapel earlier in this account, but I am tempted to restate the fact that Rosslyn Chapel was built by Sir William St. Clair, the Earl and Prince of Orkney.

Sir Walter Scott spent a lot of his time at Rosslyn, and he wrote about it, and the St. Clairs, in the "Lay of the Last Minstrel":

There are twenty Rosslyn barons bold
Lie buried within that proud chappelle
And each St. Clair was buried there
With candle, with book and with knell.

Sir William, the builder of the chapel, was the last St. Clair to be buried in the crypt, decked-out in full armor.

Returning to London we said an affectionate farewell to our chauffeur and left for Paris on July 23 to begin an exciting tour of the Continent.

At Zurich we nearly came to disaster. We decided to dismiss our car and go to Paris by fast, special-fare train. So I ordered train tickets and reservations through the hotel. The night before our departure I picked-up the long yellow envelope containing the railroad tickets. I extracted from the envelope all that I thought was necessary to get us to Paris. The next morning when we got on the train, bound first for Basel on the French border, I discovered, to my horror, I had extracted only the reserved seat tickets from the envelope, and had thrown the railroad tickets into the wastepaper basket in our hotel room.

I had only enough Swiss francs to get us to Basel, but nothing beyond that except American Express checks, which would do me no good on the train. Fortunately, after we had crossed the French border, a roly-poly French conductor came to collect tickets and I explained to him my dilemma. He good-naturedly told me to relax.

"Enjoy yourself," he said. "When we get to Paris, you wait in your seats and I will come for you and escort you to the American Express Company's office in the station. You will be able to cash whatever checks you need and pay me what you owe me." This we did.

I had frantically phoned the Zurich hotel management, as soon as I could, to ask them to look for the discarded railroad tickets, but, of course, wasn't encouraged. After we returned to the United States, I received a polite letter from the management of the Hotel Grand Dolder enclosing a check, in full, for the tickets which had been recovered.

We had returned to the United States on the Queen Mary, arriving in New York on August 19. After entertaining family and friends at dinner in New York, we drove first to Wilmington and then on to Easton. We were not to remain in Easton very long however, because very shortly we drove with Mr. and Mrs. Walter Vannerson of Wilmington, to Miami, to attend the 1958 General Convention of the Episcopal Church. This was a very interesting convention for me because my fraternity brother, and college mate, the Right Reverend Arthur Lichtenberger, Bishop of Missouri, was elected Presiding Bishop to succeed the Right Reverend Henry Knox Sherrill, who had reached the age of retirement.

Returning from Florida to Easton once again, life went less well. It was quite evident by 1959 that my dear wife was finding it increasingly difficult to walk. She had

had a number of nasty falls. I had several secret talks with our maid, Mildred Andrews, about this. We continued to consult specialists in Philadelphia.

As soon as Bishop Brooke Mosley learned of my concern, he urged me to move back to Wilmington. He said he felt we had been away from Delaware a sufficiently long time. He knew why I had gone to Easton from the Diocese of Delaware; namely, to avoid any embarrassment to myself or to him. Although we were quite reluctant to leave Easton, and our lovely home on the Peach Blossom, it did seem a wise thing to do. Our doctors in Philadelphia, Bryn Mawr and Wilmington also thought so. Therefore, in 1960 we decided to sell, and to move back to Wilmington.

This caused a great deal of unhappiness on the part of my children. They had loved Easton, and had come as often as possible to visit us. From the very beginning of our residence in Talbot County, the children and grandchildren had been most enthusiastic about Maryland.

We sold Oaklands Cottage to a retired official of the Western Electric Company on January 14, 1961. I engaged the late Walter Comegys, a well-known Easton decorator, and he took responsibility for moving and settling us in our new home in Wilmington.

At first we had thought we would build a home of our own in the country near Wilmington. However, many dear friends interceded and convinced us that the change in Mrs. McKinstry's health would seem to suggest that we live in an apartment house in the city.

We engaged a nice apartment in the Plaza, 1303 Delaware Avenue, built by the Di Sabatino family of Wilmington. After signing our contract with the Plaza, we turned to unfinished business, which included a visit to Washington to attend the 1961 inauguration as guests of the Vice-President-Elect, Lyndon B. Johnson, and his wife, Lady Bird Johnson.

On January 18, we left Easton for the Capital. We were entertained at Anderson House on Massachusetts Avenue, probably the finest mansion in Washington, and now the national headquarters of the Society of the Cincinnati.

On Thursday, January 19, we went to the reception for all the governors of the states and territories. This was held at the Sheraton-Park Hotel from three to six. While we were attending this interesting reception, a great snow storm accompanied by bitter cold winds, descended on Washington. By 6 p.m., traffic in Washington was practically at a standstill. Hundreds were marooned at the hotel.

We had invited the Reverend Donald W. Mayberry, then the rector of St. John's Church, Lafayette Square, to meet us for dinner at the Sheraton-Park, but he had telephoned that because of the snow and bitter weather, he would be unable to arrive.

So my wife and I went in to an early dinner, all alone. After dinner, we emerged from the dining room to raise questions about the weather, and we found it was even worse than before.

Facing a long evening, I sent my wife to the newstand to buy two packs of playing cards. Since I was dressed in clericals, I thought it would look more proper for my wife to be the purchaser of such items. Armed with the cards, we then went to the ballroom, where the Alabama State Society had scheduled an elaborate dinner dance. Because of the blizzard only one member of the orchestra had been able to get to the hotel, and there were no guests at all. So Mrs. Mac and I took a table in the middle of the ballroom and there we sat, playing canasta until 9:30 p.m.

At that time we went back to the main entrance of the hotel, and there I learned that occasionally a taxicab was getting through and departing with a heavy load of passengers. The snow by this time was not so heavy, but the winds were just as bitter. I gave the doorman a $5 bill and asked him to put us in the next cab. He gladly did so, but he also placed in the cab several Alabama sheriffs and they added greatly to the excitement of the evening.

We left the hotel about nine forty-five headed for Anderson House which was only a mile away. However, it took the cab until nearly midnight to get there.

All sorts of things happened en route. At one moment the Alabama sheriffs had angrily attacked the driver of another car who had refused to move his car sufficiently to let our cab through. Once we had to squeeze as close to the curb as possible to let a fire truck pass us en route to a fire. It was an unforgettable night. We were most happy to get to our beloved Anderson House, but we had to walk the last two or three blocks, facing bitter winds.

Friday, January 20, was the Inauguration. We had prominent seats reserved for us on the inaugural platform near the rostrum. Although we realized we were passing-up a great chance, and probably would never have another similar one, we decided to stay in warm Anderson House and watch the proceedings on the television.

By 8 p.m. the wind had died down considerably, and the reports came to us on television that the streets had been cleared of snow. Therefore, because my wife had spent a lot of money on the dress she intended to wear to the Inaugural Ball, we got ready and asked the butler to call a cab for us. At nine o'clock we left for the armory. We were lucky to arrive there by ten o'clock.

Since we had been assigned a box by the Vice-President, quite near the front entrance, we were able to see the guests arrive. At one point we could have touched Joseph Kennedy, father of the new President, and his wife, when they came in. About 10,000 people crowded into the armory for the Inaugural Ball.

By midnight, I had decided that we would be

smart to leave the ball before the crush, and we were able to find a taxicab and get back to Anderson House by one o'clock in the morning.

On Saturday, January 21, we returned to Easton and got through what snow was left with very little difficulty. During the following weeks at Oaklands Cottage, we packed and prepared for our departure from Talbot County.

By February 2 we were settled in our new apartment in the Plaza. Our decorator, Mr. Comegys, assisted by our faithful maid, Mildred Andrews, refused to let us enter our new home until everything was in place. Flowers filled the apartment. What a way to move! I recommend it to everyone. We were delighted with our home. The new draperies, curtains, rugs, everything was a source of delight. And, what was more important, we were back home again. This was a tremendous feeling of satisfaction.

Anxious to do as much as possible, while my Isabelle was able to get around in a limited way (she had Parkinson's disease) we motored to Paoli on February 14 from where we took the train for St. Louis, San Antonio and eventually to Los Angeles, where we visited my wife's two sisters and their husbands. Our visit to California included a pleasant time with my brother, Clarence, and his wife, who lived near San Francisco.

Chapter 27

The Bombing Episode

In mid-January 1964, my wife and I motored to Florida, stopping en route to visit friends and relatives. While at Orlando, I read in the morning paper that the striking unions on the Florida East Coast Railroad, owned by the Alfred I. du Pont estate in Florida, were allegedly dynamiting the trains and the tracks because the railroad management wouldn't surrender to their demands.

In another article in the same paper, I read a very scathing denunciation of Mrs. Alfred I. du Pont by Senator Wayne Morse of Washington, contemptuously characterizing her as a fraud in the field of philanthropies.

I sat down in a hotel room and I wrote a letter to the White House, in long hand, expressing my criticism of the alleged actions of the railroad union members, adding a denunciation of Senator Morse for his contemptuous remarks about a wonderful woman.

In my letter, I said that I had heard the railroad had requested the Justice Department in Washington, as well as the F.B.I., to come into the state to try to apprehend the dynamiters, but that the railroad had received a complete "brush-off". I said I felt a strong, embarrassing issue was emerging in Florida and that this should be brought to the attention of the President. When I finished my letter, which was five or six pages, I drove to Jacksonville for the night. It occurred to me that I might be guilty of interfering, so I telephoned Edward Ball, Mrs. du Pont's brother, who was responsible for the administration of the huge Alfred I. du Pont estate and chairman of the railroad's board of directors. I told him what I had written and asked if I should send the letter. He urged me to come at once to a quickly summoned meeting of the officers of the estate. It was to be held in his hotel suite in the Robert Myers Hotel. I agreed to be present.

When I read the letter to those attending, they were quite pleased and they asked me delay sending it until I could call at their offices in the morning, dictate it to a secretary and have copies made before mailing to the White House. I agreed, of course. By Monday noon the letter was typed and dispatched by air mail to Washington.

I had not known that President Johnson was due at the Orange Bowl in Miami that coming Friday to speak to a capacity crowd. When he came, he interrupted his prepared address, saying, "I am appalled to learn about the dynamiting of the Florida East Coast trains and railroad tracks; this is no way to settle an argument about wages. I am sending the F.B.I. into Florida in full force to apprehend the criminals guilty of this outrage."

The President did just that, and within two weeks the culprits were behind bars. Mr. Ball was particularly pleased. It is significant that there wasn't any more dynamiting on the Florida East Coast Railroad system.

It might be interesting to read the letter I wrote to Mrs. Lyndon B. Johnson. The text follows:

February 22, 1964

Dear Mrs. Johnson:
Mrs. McKinstry and I are en route home, by slow stages, after visiting many people here in Florida.
May I comment on the current feud between Senator Morse of Oregon and the Florida East Coast Railroad.
In my opinion it would be a grave mistake for the Administration to give the impression to the country that Senator Morse speaks for both the Administra-

tion and the railroad union, although the support of the latter may be thought essential to victory at the ballot box.

Mrs. Alfred I. du Pont, who is now being so ruthlessly attacked by Senator Morse, is loved by many thousands of alumni of numerous colleges and universities in the south, because of her wonderful generosity. The Bishop of Virginia will confirm my statement that literally thousands of successful men and women in this nation have won their education and fame because Mrs. du Pont helped to educate them. Mr. Rice, president of the Atlantic Coast Line Railroad, is one of these, and will eloquently testify to this wonderful lady's generosity.

Alumni so respect and love her, that on several prominent university campuses, one will find a Jessie Ball du Pont Chapel; or, a new college library bearing her name—or, again, a college dormitory, etc. No woman in this country has more honorary degrees. Certainly I know of no one who has given more widely to college endowments.

No wonder Her Majesty, the Queen of England, in 1963, bestowed upon Mrs. du Pont the highest honor, because of her generosity in England as well as in America.

Today, because of poor health, Mrs. du Pont is pretty much confined to her home. Does Senator Morse realize the storm he is about to create, by his attack and misrepresentations, in regard to Mrs. du Pont and her alleged lack of generosity? College alumni and citizens in the south will not forget this and will rally to her cause and side. In talking with many people in Florida, I find this is true. There is a growing indignation which should be noted.

I find that many people suspect the attack on Mrs. du Pont by Senator Morse, and the bombing of trains en route to Florida are largely due to the rage and anger of the railroad unions levelled against the FEC for positively reproving the foolishness of 'featherbedding'. Please read the February 22 issue of the Saturday Evening Post. It deserves careful study.

If the people on the sidelines suspect that the Secretary of Labor or Senator Morse (I devoutly and confidently hope not the Administration) are being unfair to Mrs. du Pont; if the public sees in the failure of the F.B.I. to find the agents or persons guilty of serious sabotage to the FEC an attempt to pander to the unions; and should the people become increasingly suspicious that the FEC is being used by the railroad unions as a 'whipping boy' because the road has eliminated 'featherbedding', all this could become a campaign issue, especially in Florida.

However, my main reason for writing is to express my deep indignation over the things Senator Morse has said about Mrs. du Pont, and also, to express the hope that the President will in no way give support to all this. Senator Morse may indeed be sorry before he is through.

The FEC seems to me to have sound fiscal reasons for not being able to afford the total increase in wages demanded by the National Railroad Unions. The loss of Cuban business and the Bay of Pigs fiasco only further hurt the road's hopes for the future. However, I am no authority on railroads. But this I do know—never, never make the mistake in the South, or in the North either, of spreading false facts against Mrs. Alfred I. du Pont, one of the great and generous souls in our world. (Can't you warn Senator Morse somehow to be a bit more temperate?)

Our compliments to the President and yourself.

Sincerely yours,
Arthur R. McKinstry

Chapter 28

Personal Matters

Problems of health really began to plague us both, my wife and me, as we entered the era of the middle 1960's.

Mrs. Mac was losing the free use of her limbs, and more and more she felt the need of a wheelchair. Parkinson's disease is a relentless foe.

On the advice of specialists in Philadelphia, we undertook one more trip to Florida in early January, 1965. I had engaged a good driver to take us to Delray, where we would be guests at the oceanside home of Mr. and Mrs. J. Bruce Bredin who had so generously turned over their beautiful estate to us for this vacation.

I might add that the Bredins had done things like that for us for years. My daughter, Mrs. Paul P. Lawton, and her daughter, Carolyn, accompanied us on this trip. It was with considerable difficulty that we reached our destination at Delray because of my wife's condition. More than once we devoutly wished we had never started on that journey.

This stay was soon marred by a severe accident. While I was out of the bedroom early one morning, my wife got out of her bed and attempted to walk. She fell, hitting the back of her head on a sharp dresser drawer.

The doctors rushed her by ambulance to the hospital in Boynton Beach. Emergency care was followed by several weeks in a nursing home there. Finally, on February 1, 1965, we took Isabelle by ambulance to the Miami Airport, accompanied by a very resourceful nurse. She was flown back to Philadelphia and then driven to the

Eugene du Pont Convalescent Hospital near Wilmington, where she stayed for many weeks.

My son, Jim, flew to Jacksonville to meet me and took over the driving, inasmuch as we had released our driver as soon as we had arrived in Delray. Jim drove me back to Wilmington. I must say this last trip had been a most unfortunate one.

However, within a few weeks, Mrs. Mac was back in the Plaza again and everything was going as well as possible under the circumstances. The doctor prescribed nursing for my wife and we had the help of two very good maids.

I was determined to keep going as long as possible, and to give my dear wife as good a time as I could. Therefore, three or four days a week, the nurse and a maid would wheel her down to the Plaza entrance in a wheelchair, put her in my car and the wheelchair in the trunk. We would motor an hour or so to some restaurant in Delaware or in nearby Pennsylvania. I made it my business to know every good restaurant within fifty miles of Wilmington, especially those where a wheelchair would not confront stairways.

We enjoyed our rides together. I knew, of course, that the time would soon come when Isabelle would be unable to take even short trips of this type. Therefore, I made the most of every opportunity. I devoted each day to her and to her wishes and, I might add, she was always the most congenial, uncomplaining companion.

She loved our apartment in the Plaza, and on the whole she was quite comfortable, thanks to Mrs. Evelyn Harkins, our nurse, and Evelyn and Margaret, our maids. Time passed.

Then on May 27, 1966, Doctor Lewis Flinn ordered an ambulance and my wife was rushed to the Exeter Hall Nursing Home on the Lancaster Pike following a slight stroke.

In the meantime, I maintained the apartment in

the Plaza, assisted by maids. But it was a very lonely life without my wife.

One day in August, I was seated in the lobby of the Hotel Du Pont, feeling quite sorry for myself. The Reverend Doctor George H. Pigueron, Jr., an old friend, came into the lobby, spied me and asked, "Why do you look so downhearted?"

I told him my story. Doctor Pigueron, the builder and administrator of the Methodist Country House opposite the new Wilmington Country Club on the Kennett Pike, expressed his sympathy and asked me if I would call on him at the Country House the next day. I did so.

He showed me through the fabulous building and we looked in the infirmary, which is one of the best in the country. He then told me that he had a plan. He wanted me to move to the Country House in September.

He took me to quarters which he said were available to me. He explained that, of course, I would have to pay for the quarters, but he would be very happy to have me come. He added, "Whenever Dr. Flinn thinks it feasible we would be very glad to have your wife move from Exeter Hall into the infirmary."

I asked him why he was being so generous to me. He then reminded me I had always been a strong supporter of the Methodist Country House and had encouraged members of the Episcopal Church, who could affort it, to give generously towards its construction and maintenance. He was generous enough to say that the House would not have been possible without the help of the communicants of the Episcopal Church, who had put up at least two-thirds of the money.

He said, "I feel we owe a debt to the Episcopal Church, and I want to show my gratitude by inviting you to come here to live with us."

I asked him to give me a week's time in which to consider the matter. I discussed the subject with my own doctors and my wife's physicians—with my children and with a few friends. Finally I decided this was the thing to do, and I accepted Doctor Pigueron's very kind offer.

It was now necessary for me to engage interior decorators to tell me what I would need by way of draperies, rugs and furniture (from our apartment). When this was decided, I spent weeks dividing the remainder of the furnishings at the Plaza. I tried to be as just and fair as I could as I dispatched items to my five children in Wilmington, Massachusetts and Florida.

On September 1, 1966, the vans moved me to the Methodist Country House and took the surplus furniture, silver and furnishings to my children. My decorators had me settled in my small new quarters that afternoon. So began another chapter in my rather interesting life.

At the Methodist Country House I found many old friends. Among them were Mr. and Mrs. J. Edgar Rhoads, Mr. and Mrs. Alva E. Lindley and Miss Blanche Swayne. There were over 200 residents in the House; some were people with ample means, others were there almost on full "scholarships". I discovered that the entire group were good neighbors and willing to be good friends.

The Country House, I found, was efficiently run, and the housekeeping was immaculate. The people of Wilmington can be proud of the place. I feel the community should be greatly indebted to Dr. Pigueron, the man who conceived the idea and who, with the help of generous people in Wilmington, brought his dream to fruition. I have now been a resident there for over eight years, and I have found not only great peace of mind, but also many benefits from my contacts with the members of the House.

The Country House is a wonderful place to be in times of illness. For example, I had known since the summer of 1966 that I faced a plastic surgery operation early in 1967. Physicians had discovered a pre-cancerous condition on my lower lip, and this had to be eliminated as soon as possible. Undoubtedly this condition had been aggravated in earlier years by smoking cigars. Of course, I gave up smoking a long time ago, but the damage had been done.

In years past I had been threatened with surgery, but, somehow I had been able to outwit my surgeons and escape. For instance about 1935, while I was a resident of San Antonio, my throat specialist there insisted that he be permitted to remove my tonsils. It is true that when I was foolish enough to preach twenty-five minutes in my church in San Antonio, a building which was noted for its poor acoustics, my throat would get quite hoarse, and my voice noticeably weakened. Therefore, my specialist was convinced the removal of my tonsils would correct this condition. Fortunately for me, another specialist, a doctor at the Fort Sam Houston Hospital, and a dear friend, was just as sure my tonsils should not be cut out.

While these two medics argued back and forth over my condition, I gathered my wife and children together and sneaked out of the city. I headed for our summer home, "Meadowmere", thirty miles north of Boston. Arriving there, my wife and I went to a tea the next afternoon at a home in the neighborhood. There we met Mrs. Eames, the mother of the headmaster of the famous Governor Dummer Academy nearby. Mrs. Eames told me the shocking news that her son Ted, the well-known headmaster, was going to have his tonsils removed the following week. He had engaged a famous Harvard Medical School doctor to do the job, in the hospital at Newburyport. As usual I talked too much, and I confided in Mrs. Eames that I had just escaped a like operation while two specialists were tied up in heated argument about my condition.

To my great consternation, Mrs. Eames, one of those grand dames who talks more than she listens, ignored my feeling of jubilation over my escape from torture. When she returned to her son's house, she informed him that I, too, would like to have my tonsils removed at the same time he had his taken out.

I was terribly upset when Mr. Eames telephoned me the next morning to tell me how happy he was that I would be joining him at the Newburyport hospital. I stammered some sort of weak alibi to the effect that I couldn't possibly consider such a thing without consulting my summer physician.

"Who is he?" asked Ted Eames.

I replied, "Dr. Bullard of Newburyport."

I was amazed to have him reply that Dr. Bullard was his physician and the one who was about to engineer his operation! Between Mr. Eames and my family, I was badgered into consulting Dr. Bullard, who, after examining my poor tonsils with mirrors, cautiously refrained from an opinion of his own. He insisted that I meet Dr. Schall of Harvard, who would arrive the next day for the purpose of operating on Ted Eames. I was ordered to go into the hospital for a consultation with Dr. Schall.

I slept very little that night. I woke-up several times wondering why I was so weak. "Am I a man or a mouse?"

The next day, I met Dr. Schall just after I had seen Ted Eames wheeled past, dead to the world, headed for the torture chamber. The doctor asked me if I knew his friend, Bishop Henry Knox Sherrill of Massachusetts, and I declared that I did. He then used mirrors to examine my tonsils, after which he asked me, "Tell me, why do you want me to take them out?"

I assured the doctor I had no such desire. I told him about my doctors in San Antonio and how they disagreed. I told him also that my specialist had advised the operation because my voice grew hoarse and was noticeably weaker after I preached for twenty-five minutes.

Dr. Schall evidently liked to tease. He informed

me that his fee was considered by many people to be rather large. He said he would be very happy to operate on me if I were sick. But his personal advice to me was that henceforth I preach but eighteen minutes and keep my tonsils! A great load was lifted from my mind, my heart, my pocketbook and my tonsils. That night I really celebrated my escape!

Years later, the Cleveland Clinic discovered that I had some dear little gall stones, which, in the clinic's opinion, should be watched but not at that time operated upon. I returned to Wilmington and soon reported to my doctors at the University of Pennsylvania Hospital. I told them about my experience in Cleveland.

They, in turn, conferred with the famous Dr. Ravdin, chief of surgery there. He asked me to come into the hospital after he had secured the pictures of the gall stones from the Cleveland Clinic. Together, the doctors studied the pictures, and they ordered me to have an operation.

I demurred by inquiring, "How many people on whom you operate for gall stones know far in advance— never having had any trouble—that they have those dear little stones inside them?" Dr. Ravdin replied, "Very few." I pursued the subject further.

"How many of your patients recover after an operation for gall stones?"

"Why, practically all of them."

"Well, what have I got to lose if I wait until I have an attack, or at least have felt some symptoms?"

I announced I was returning to my bed and board in Wilmington, and I promptly left the hospital and my medics, the latter a bit disgusted with me. I still have my gall stones and they have never bothered me.

So when I was told that I faced plastic surgery and a new lower lip, I began to squirm. How could I get out of this one? As time went on, and I had frequent consultations with the plastic surgeon in Bryn Mawr, I recalled my freshman days in college. A fellow freshman, who was a great football player but who had had little cultural background, entitled his first freshman theme in the English course "And the Train Came Rushing Down the Track with No Way Out". I realized there would be no way out for me this time.

Consequently, on Monday, January 9, 1967, I was driven to the Bryn Mawr Hospital for my plastic operation. My dear friend, the Reverend Doctor John W. Christie, accompanied me. After depositing me there, he returned to Wilmington leaving me alone to face my operation.

After the usual preparations the night before, I was wheeled to the operating room at 8 a.m., the next day. My internist, Dr. W. W. Dyer, was delayed in arriving and had no opportunity to persuade the surgeon to eliminate adrenalin from the anesthetic which he administered to me. Before the operation could actually begin I had such a violent reaction that my blood pressure fell about forty points in a second or two, and I perspired bucketsful. The surgeon and his assistants became quite alarmed and they quickly called off the operation and rushed me to the oxygen tents for recovery. (I always did like a commotion.)

In due time, I was wheeled back to my room, feeling somewhat defeated, and I remained there until I fully recovered and until the doctors could agree among themselves as to what had gone wrong.

When my internist came to my bedside to visit, he was most apologetic for having failed to arrive at the beginning of the operation. He explained the trouble was due, in his opinion, to the fact that the anesthetic had included some adrenalin which should never be given to a diabetic. Dr. Dyer had difficulty convincing the surgeon and the heart specialists of this fact, however.

Two days later, minus the adrenalin, the operation was a success. I now had a new lower lip. By 1968 I knew the operation was a complete success, except for the fact that I can no longer pucker and kiss as I once did.

On January 21, I returned to the Methodist Country House. I went inside to discover that during my absence from the Country House Dr. Pigueron and Dr. Flinn had removed my wife from Exeter Hall on Lancaster Pike to the infirmary at the Country House. It was indeed a wonderful reunion for us, and I was grateful to God that once more we were together under the same roof, even though she would have to live in the infirmary, an "eighth of a mile" down the hall.

Three wonderful nurses looked after her during the time of her illness and through to the very end. They were Mrs. Evelyn Harkins, who had been with us from the beginning of her illness, assisted by Mrs. Virginia Jones and Mrs. Constance Rucker, who in the years past had been of wonderful assistance to us when we kept house. No person could have had more loyal and devoted nursing. They served her faithfully.

My dear Isabelle lived in the infirmary of the Methodist Country House from January, 1967, until late October, 1971, when she peacefully passed from this limited sphere into life eternal. She had been ill since 1960, seriously so since 1964. By 1970 she had become completely helpless. But all through her illness she had been perfectly wonderful. She had great poise, and she never complained. She was descended from the Van Doorns of Castle Doorn in Holland, from the English Early family of Witney, England, famous woolen merchants, and from the Van Dorns of Cleveland, who were iron and steel people. They had also founded the first electric tool business in this country, a company which merged just before the stock crash of 1929 with Black and Decker of Baltimore. She had had a wonderful background and she gave honor to it by her personality and her great charm.

Before I cease to think and speak of the situation

in which my wife and I had been situated, I do want to pay tribute to our wonderful children, who greatly sustained us in every difficulty. It was fortunate for us we had two of our children living in Wilmington. They and their families were of constant help and support. I mentioned Mrs. Paul P. Lawton and her husband and daughter Carolyn, and my son James T. McKinstry, his wife, Jane, and their three beautiful children, Thomas, Susan and Karen. What an inspiration they have been to us through the years.

All families tend to scatter somewhat, and so its no surprise that my first daughter, Isabelle Van Dorn Stadler, lives in Florida, actually in Orange Park south of Jacksonville, in a home alongside the water. Her husband left the Navy to enter the banking business. They have lived there with their four children: Isabelle (known as Kippy) now graduated from college; Paul, Jr., now a student at Stetson University; Donald Early about to go to college in the fall of 1974, and James Arthur, still in Jacksonville schools.

Farther down Florida, at Lake Wales, my son Arthur lives with his wonderful wife, Elaine, a musician and psychologist—and their two children, Kevin and Tracy. Arthur and his wife are giving their life and strength to maladjusted children who attend the Vanguard School in Lake Wales.

My second daughter, Mrs. John C. Maull, does not live too far away. She and her husband and three children, Margaret Adelaide, John McKinstry and Elizabeth Ann, live in the town of Uxbridge, near Worcester, Massachusetts.

These wonderful children and grandchildren have been a great source of help and inspiration, especially at the time of my dear Isabelle's death.

Although now the strain of Isabelle's long illness was lifted and I was happy for her that the struggle was over, still I was extremely lonely. There was much to do, of course, in the settling of her estate. When that was successfully concluded, my three daughters, Isabelle, Margaret and Barbara, decided to take me to the British Isles in the summer of 1972. We had a wonderful time motoring in Ireland, Scotland and England. In fact, I was so lifted-up by my experience that I explained to them, "Girls, I think I must have actually been starved for good feminine companionship."

This led the girls to ask if I did not think I would remarry sometime if I found someone with whom I could be thoroughly happy and contented. In fact they began to make a few suggestions. These I rejected. And finally I said to them, "Girls, I think I know a wonderful woman, someone whom you love very much, who has been a dear and close friend of our family since we came to Delaware more than thirty-five years ago."

The more I thought about it, the more the idea interested me. I began to write to this lady while I was still in the British Isles—just casual notes.

Returning to Wilmington, I saw something of this lovely churchwoman. We drove to Atlantic City one day for a walk on the Boardwalk, and her conversation was so delightful and inspiring that re-marriage began to attract my attention. I dislike being alone. I had been so alone for so long a time.

I refer, of course, to Mrs. Margery Robinson Vannerson, whose husband, Walter, had long been associated with the Du Pont Company and later with Hercules. He had been a friend of mine, and had died two months following Isabelle's death, in 1971.

Finally, I told my family of the possibility, and they were delighted because they had long adored Margery. Robert Vannerson, her son, had been my boy Jim's best friend in school days. Her daughter, Jane, had been a particular pet of mine, and I had been instrumental in getting Mrs. Alfred I. du Pont to give her a generous scholarship when she went to college. Both of her children were

Back Row: L. to R., Paul Lawton, Arthur S. McKinstry, Arthur R. McKinstry, James T. McKinstry, Cdr. Paul C. Stadler, John C. Maull

Middle Row: L. to R., Jane McKinstry, Thomas McKinstry, Barbara Lawton, Isabelle McKinstry, Margaret Maull, Elaine McKinstry, Isabelle Stadler, James Stadler

Front Row: L. to R., Elizabeth Maull, Isabelle Stadler, Kevin McKinstry, Margaret Maull, Donald Stadler, Tracy McKinstry, Paul Stadler, John Maull, Carolyn Lawton extremely able and attractive, and friends of my own children.

Margery's ancestory has lived in Wilmington, indeed many of them were buried from Old Swedes' Church, and in that churchyard there are numerous graves testifying to her connection with early Wilmington. In her youth, before her first marriage, she was a very well known school teacher, and it has been interesting to me to see how often former pupils have rushed to her, throwing their arms around her neck exclaiming, "My favorite teacher!"

After I proposed to her, she consulted her own family and found they were extremely happy over the prospects and gave their complete blessing.

We became engaged, but kept this a closely guarded secret not to be revealed by family until after the day of our marriage, which took place on January 6, 1973 in Bishopstead Chapel. The marriage service was conducted by William H. Mead, then the Bishop of Delaware. It began with a communion service at eleven o'clock. Bishop Andrew Y. Y. Tsu and the Reverend Doctor John W. Christie, both my dear friends, assisted in the communion service, and Bishop Mead presided over the marriage ceremony, attended also by several of my grandchildren.

[236]

Following the wedding ceremony, Bishop Mead and his wife gave a pleasant reception at Bishopstead which was attended by family and a few close friends. Then I gave a "wedding breakfast" for the bride and members of the family at the Wilmington Country Club. During that affair, Walter S. Carpenter, Jr., came up the stairs into the room, kissed the bride, congratulated me most heartily saying, "You have done the right thing." He was a most enthusiastic supporter and always had been a dear friend of mine.

Soon we were on our way to Florida, where we

had two beautiful weeks at the Bredin home at Delray Beach, followed by a cruise in the West Indies. Returning to Florida, we spent a few days in Miami and Boca Grande, returning to Jacksonville to visit family.

We then flew to San Antonio, where we had front page publicity and a most joyous welcome from old friends. We were swamped with invitations to breakfast, lunch and dinner. We had expected to visit Mrs. Lyndon B. Johnson at the LBJ Ranch, but because her husband had recently died she was busy with the thousands of messages of condolence she thought she should answer. We decided not to go to see her. Later, when we returned to Wilmington, we found a letter from her chastising us for passing her up. We really should have gone, but the visit was only postponed.

On March 1, 1973, Margery and I moved into the Methodist Country House into my apartment, which she preferred to anything else. A tea was given in her honor that day at the Country House so as to give her an [237] opportunity to meet the residents. She knew a surprisingly large number of them, or at least friends and relatives of theirs. She was warmly received from the start and has fitted into the place most remarkably. Soon she was completely at home.

Our marriage has given me an enormous lift. No more loneliness for either of us. She has a wonderful mind. She knows the church almost as well as I do and she knows the Prayer Book by heart. She likes to travel, as I do. And best of all, her children and grandchildren are good friends of all of mine. The grandchildren in the two families number nineteen. When we add to that number seven children with spouses, we have a glorious total of thirty-three. A very congenial and happy family. May it continue this way as long as the good Lord permits.

Margery's grandchildren are Thomas A. McKenna, Jr., Carol Lee McKenna and Douglas Bradford

McKenna, all children of her daughter Jane, who was married to Thomas A. McKenna, an honored employee of the Du Pont Company.

The children of her son, Robert Aglmer Vannerson, who lives with his wife, Alice, in Sudsbury, Massachusetts, are Stephen Huntington, Stuart Harris and Mollie Sherwood.

Chapter 29

Kelso's "Chaplain"

One of my perpetual fears was that, as a Bishop, I would not find opportunity to be a pastor. This proved groundless. Not only did I serve as pastor to many people through the years but, Heaven save us, I also became chaplain for Kelso, five times named Horse of the Year and winner of more money than any other race horse in history.

I was brought up with horses as a youth on my family's farms in Kansas. Later, during our residence in San Antonio from 1931 until 1938, I was permitted the use of a 10,000 acre ranch for the summer vacations of my family and friends. There were fifty saddle horses to be ridden on whim.

When Kelso, owned by Mrs. Richard C. du Pont, began to attract the attention of racing fans throughout the nation, I became one of the most ardent among them. The animal fascinated me and I watched him race whenever I could.

There was a discernible difference between Kelso and other horses. I noted that when other mounts were being brought from the barns by their grooms they walked along with their heads down in a mechanical, docile way. Kelso, on the other hand, would consistently pull away from his groom and go to the fence where the crowds had gathered. There he would sniff the outstretched hands and, I think, talk to the throng as he walked slowly to the paddock. Kelso I suspect was himself "people". There's no doubt he cast a spell over all crowds at all race tracks. His popularity was such that he was protected, in some paddock areas, by three or four guards.

In 1965, I went to Saratoga to watch him run in the Whitney Stakes race. I took my son, Jim, and his wife, Jane, with me. We were given the box of George H. Humphreys, Secretary of the Treasury, and very good seats they were. The minute Kelso won this exciting race, I ran down the aisle to congratulate Mrs. duPont, who was jumping up and down like a cricket in her excitement. She embraced me and said, "Come on, Bishop Mac, you and Jim and Jane must accompany me to the winner's circle."

We hurried down the stairs and out the door where the Saratoga uniformed employees of the race track had formed an honor guard for the "Queen of the Day", Mrs. duPont. We went to the winner's circle—the crowds in the stand were still standing and cheering the winner and his jockey, and, of course, the owner.

When the noise subsided, Mrs. duPont presented me to Mr. Whitney and over the microphone to the crowds. My astonished ears heard Mrs. duPont say, "This is Bishop McKinstry of Delaware, who is Kelso's chaplain."

This caused quite a ripple among the hard-boiled newspapermen. And when the chance came some reporters got me aside saying, "Kelso's chaplain? What did she mean?"

I replied, "You gentlemen will agree that there is a strange affinity between the spiritual and the beautiful, won't you?"

They looked somewhat confused but were willing to accept this premise.

"Well then, look at Kelso. Isn't he beautiful? Of *course* he needs a chaplain."

The next issue of *Sports Illustrated* carried an article titled, "Faith and Form at Saratoga" by Whitney

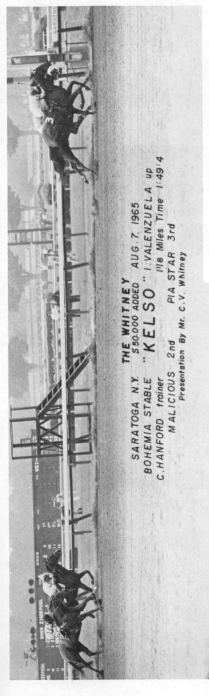

Kelso wins The Whitney. Sports Illustrated carries the story of horse, owner and "Chaplain"

THE WHITNEY
$50,000 ADDED   AUG.7.1965
SARATOGA N.Y.
BOHEMIA STABLE "KELSO" I·VALENZUELA up
C.HANFORD trainer   1⅛ Miles Time 1:49·4
MALICIOUS 2nd   PIA STAR 3rd
Presentation By Mr. C.V. Whitney

FAITH AND FORM AT SARATOGA

The first was shown by a bishop singular for his trackside intercession in behalf of a superhorse, the second by Kelso himself, who has now proved his superiority over six racing crops and 70,000 rivals   **by WHITNEY TOWER**

Not being a horseplayer of international renown, the kindly-faced man with graying hair was inconspicuous among the 23,560 persons who showed up Saturday to watch the Whitney Stakes at Saratoga. The Right Reverend Arthur R. McKinstry, retired Episcopal Bishop of Delaware, was attired in a plain business suit, and in truth he was not a model of clerical calm as he stood elbow to elbow with a mob that, pushing into the beautiful saddling enclosure, almost detached the stirrups from their recots. (Officials, while acknowledging that Saratoga had put more people in the stands, estimated that at least 12,000 of them jammed into the paddock area to look at Kelso, the hero of the decade. Not since Native Dancer performed as a 3-year-old had the old track seen such a crush.) On the contrary, Bishop McKinstry freely admitted to a spattering of goose pimples, which is quite an admission for the man who officiated at the marriage of President Lyndon B. Johnson.

"On the occasion of President and Mrs. Johnson's 30th wedding anniversary," said the bishop, "the White House reporters asked me if I had any other claim to fame. I thought a little while and then had to confess to them that among my friends in Wilmington I am casually spoken of as the private chaplain for that great racehorse Kelso. Taken aback, one reporter turned and asked me, 'Do you mean to say that you direct heavenly words to God on behalf of a racehorse?' 'I don't have to,' I replied. 'Let's say I just sit there with my fingers crossed and hope a little.' "

Bishop McKinstry, as it turned out, he recalls, "was crying and then praying." When Kelso runs that I feel I'm trying to recite the Greek alphabet backward to take my mind off things."

There's no telling how many alphabets the good bishop recited last Saturday —or in precisely what order he chose to rattle them off—but it's a safe bet that from the quarter pole to the finish line,

which is exactly where Kelso nipped Malicious by a nose to win the Whitney, his Heaven-directed output of the right words would have made all loyal Delaware churchgoers proud. They can be assured that their man in Saratoga helped Kelso get the job done.

Mrs. Richard C. duPont's ageless gelding has demonstrated his superiority over six racing crops totaling more than 70,000 horses, and this 36th running of the Whitney was about as workmanlike a performance as a top horse when he won the Whitney back in 1961. When he gained the victory in 1963, at the age of six. Now, at 8, he is unique—an athlete like Ruth, Tilden, Hitchcock, Dempsey or Bobby Jones who combines all the skills of his profession with a personal magnetism that a movie star might envy.

In Kelso's last race, the Brooklyn Handicap, where he had to give away 11 pounds to Pia Star and Roman Brother,

Tower. I quote from the August 16, 1965 number of that magazine:

Not being a horse player of international renown, the kindly faced man with graying hair was inconspicuous among the 23,360 persons who showed up Saturday to watch the Whitney Stakes at Saratoga. The Right Reverend Arthur R. McKinstry, retired Episcopal Bishop of Delaware, was attired in a plain business suit, and in truth he was not a model of clerical calm as he stood elbow to elbow with a mob that, pushing into the beautiful saddling enclosure, almost detached the elms from their roots. (Officials, while acknowledging that Saratoga had put more people in the stands, estimated that at least 12,000 of them jammed into the paddock area to look at Kelso, the hero of the decade. Not since Native Dancer performed as a three year old had the old track seen such a crush.) On the contrary, Bishop McKinstry freely admitted to a spattering of goose-pimples, which is quite an admission for the man who officiated at the marriage of President Lyndon B. Johnson.

[242]

Bishop McKinstry admitted that when Kelso runs, "Actually, I get so nervous that I feel like trying to recite the Greek alphabet backward to take my mind off things."

There's no telling how many alphabets the good Bishop recited last Saturday—or in precisely what order he chose to rattle them off—but it's a safe bet that from the quarter pole to the finish line, which is exactly where Kelso nipped Malicious by a nose to win the Whitney, his Heaven-directed output of the right words would have made all loyal Delaware churchgoers proud. They can be assured that their man in Saratoga helped Kelso get the job done.

Not to be outdone, the *Philadelphia Evening Bulletin* sent a feature writer and a photographer to my

Bishop McKinstry and Mrs. Richard C. duPont at the opening of The Kelso Room, Aqueduct Race Track—1966

apartment in the Plaza in Wilmington to concoct a special article for the newspaper's Sunday magazine. The author of the article, dated November 28, 1965, was Joseph F. Lowry. It began:

Like most other millionaires, Kelso, perhaps the greatest horse—up to this time—has everything. He eats his own specially packaged brand of sugar cubes, drinks Arkansas spring water costing $1 a jug, gets ice cream for dessert, wears a silver mink collar in his stall, sleeps on a bed of sugar cane fibers, has his own mail box, races with a ribbon in his hair, and he has a Bishop for a chaplain.

I said to the author of the Bulletin article: "Yes, my friends call me Kelso's chaplain. But please get this straight, I did not renounce my ministry to do this for Kelso. I just love that horse. Goodness no, I do not bet. Neither does the owner of Kelso, Mrs. Richard duPont."

[244]   It was thus that my ministry was enlarged, and I became Kelso's chaplain. When he retired from the track I made it my responsibility to call on him occasionally, and hear his confession if he cared to make one. He never did.

I had a feeler from another famous stable, after Kelso's retirement, asking if I would care to take on another great horse. I politely declined, saying I was entirely too busy looking after people. Furthermore, in my opinion no horse could equal my Kelso.

If St. Francis of Assisi could have his birds to shepherd, why couldn't I have Kelso? People, birds and horses live under the same God who created them. A pastor should be interested in all living things—including people and horses. So be it!

Chapter 30

First Philadelphia City Troop

In 1972, through the auspices of my dear friend Robert N. Downs, III, I became involved with one of the country's most illustrious military organizations, The First Philadelphia City Troop.

This famous cavalry unit was founded in 1774. Mr. Downs, one of the great layman of the Diocese of Delaware, is Senior Honorary Captain of the City Troop.

One day, Bob Downs asked me to go with him to the City Troop's Fall Banquet. I was pleased to be invited and accepted with enthusiasm.

At the armory in Philadelphia, I mingled with the Troopers at a reception, and noted that their numbers included a great many of the most prominent business and society figures in Philadelphia. We awaited the arrival of the mounted members of the Troop. As they rode up in formation I went out to watch their entrance, and once again was inspired with the beauty of uniformed men astride magnificent steeds.

Later, we gathered on the top floor of the armory in the banquet hall and I found myself at the head table near Captain Downs. There was no grace before meat because it was never the tradition of the organization to have grace. Also at the head table were various Captains of the Troop and many distinguished guests, including Generals and Admirals from the Army and the Navy.

When the dinner was over, Captain Dawson,

rose to introduce those seated at the head table. When he came to me, he said, "We will pass by this guest for the moment." When he had presented the Senior Honorary Captain, Robert Downs, the latter proceeded to spring a surprise on me. He introduced me to the Troop, saying, "Gentlemen of the Troop, this organization was founded, as you well know, in the year 1774. The Troop has never had the honor of a chaplain. We have served this country in wars and emergencies down through the years and with great success. But we've never had a chaplain."

He continued, "It is my great honor tonight to inform you that, with the approval of those in authority, I have the high honor of nominating the Right Reverend Arthur R. McKinstry, the retired Bishop of Delaware, to be the first chaplain of this distinguished organization. I ask your approval."

[246] There was great applause. The Troop members rose to their feet and they burst into song (some of the lyrics, I must add, being somewhat naughty). When the singing stopped and I was able to reply, I did so:

"Captain Downs, Captain Dawson, distinguished guests and members of this great organization. I am completely taken by surprise. I had no idea that this would happen to me. I am deeply moved by this honor. The warmth of your welcome, as well as your magnificent singing moves me greatly."

I then spoke about my love for Philadelphia and about some of my dearest friends, who had been Philadelphians of distinction—including the late George Wharton Pepper, with whom I had served on the chapter of the Washington Cathedral for many years. I reminded them I had given Senator Pepper a dinner in Philadelphia many years ago, and it had been attended by some of those present. It was most propitious that I mentioned Senator Pepper, as some of his relatives and descendants were present at the banquet that night. Then I continued:

"But gentlemen—I am an absentee Bishop. I live

Bishop McKinstry, Chaplain to The First City Troop (inset) A platoon of the Troop at 4th & Chestnut Streets, Philadelphia

in Wilmington. More than that, I am a retired Bishop. Do you know what a retired Bishop is? A retired Bishop is one who gets up at eight o'clock in the morning, puts the cat out, brings in the morning papers, sits down quickly and reads the obituaries. And if he's not listed there he goes back to bed again."

I said, "As I look over this wonderful group of people here tonight, and listen to your songs, I can't help but wonder whether down deep in your hearts you have a longing for salvation. Do you really feel, deep down, that you are in such need? If so, don't you think it would be much smarter for you to elect a local character, somebody who lives amongst you, somebody who can snoop into your personal affairs and see what you are up to? But, sirs, if you honestly feel down deep in your hearts that you are in no immediate need of salvation, then, undoubtedly, I am your man."

This facetious little speech of mine was met by enormous applause and again by wonderful singing, and although the ten minutes of singing included a few more ribald songs, the spirit was magnificent.

Following this surprising event, I was properly decked out with a splendid uniform, which I have worn to all subsequent banquets. And, whereas it had never been the custom through the long history of this organization to have grace before meat, I note that now the captain says, "We will call upon our chaplain to say grace."

I am deeply indebted to Senior Honorary Captain Robert N. Downs, III, and to Captain Dawson and Captain Bright for honoring me so highly in my advanced years.

Another of my duties as chaplain of the First City Troop has been to deliver the sermon at the annual service commemorating the anniversary of George Washington's death.

On December 16, 1973 we met at old St. Peter's Church on a gray, miserable day. In spite of a severe blizzard, the Troop arrived as scheduled, resplendent on their magnificent horses. The service was most impressive. I was accompanied by Margery, my son Jim and his wife Jane—and their son, Tommy.

Jim had brought a tape recorder with him, and in his high box-pew, not far from the pulpit, he was able to record the entire service.

At the second such service I attended, the weather and the scene had changed.

The reader may be interested in my remarks delivered December 15, 1974 at Christ Church, Philadelphia. Following is my exhortation:

"On this historic occasion, when we are met here

Sergeant Robert N. Downs III, First City Troop—1930

to remember the 175th anniversary of the passing of George Washington from this life, let us consider the Trinity of life's fundamental attitudes which seem, to me at least, to be the foundation stones of the life and leadership of General Washington.

"We find these fundamental attitudes expressed in the book of the Prophet Ezekiel:

"Chapter 1, Verse 28: *And when I saw it—I fell upon my face.*

"Chapter 2, Verse 1: *And he said unto me, 'Son of man—stand upon thy feet.'*

"Chapter 3, Verse 15: *I sat where they sat.*

"When the Continental Congress, meeting

within the shadow of Christ Church, selected George Washington as Commander-in-Chief of the Colonial forces soon to be enlisted and trained for war, the First Troop promptly reported to Washington, and offered to serve as his bodyguard, and go with him on his first military campaigns. It is not difficult for us here today to imagine the tremendous sense of satisfaction which Washington must have felt when he realized the great importance of Captain Markoe's formation of this Troop.

"It is common for some people in our cynical era to try to explain outstanding, constructive events in life—events for which there seems to be no logical explanation—as merely accidental. But there are others of us who believe that such great and beneficially constructive acts are Providential, not mere accidents. By Providential, we mean that such acts were inspired by the All-Wise Architect of our world—Almighty God Himself.

[250] "To Abraham Markoe, a Danish citizen living in Philadelphia at the time, it was given to see the coming of a war between England and the nearly defenseless Colonies. And knowing that there was at that time no formal military organization in existence, Markoe promptly brought the First Troop into being. He trained its able members for military action. As you well know, the King of Denmark ultimately realized the implications of all this, and he ordered his subject—Markoe—to resign from the Troop so as to avoid involving Denmark, in the event that war between England and the Colonies should come to pass. But immediately, one of the Troop's illustrious members, Captain Morris, took over the command, and he soon waited upon Washington, presenting the new Commander-in-Chief with a cavalry Troop that was disciplined, self-financed, composed of men of outstanding character and deep loyalty and ready for service in the first months of one of the most crucial military campaigns in history.

"It is well known that the Troop served with great devotion and sacrifice. It is recorded that following the Battle of Trenton, members of the Troop were on duty two nights and a day, without adequate food and without sleep. They were indeed loyal to the cause of freedom.

"But there was, I think, another ingredient that helped to elicit such sacrificial devotion. What was that something more that prompted the Troop to raise large sums of money, which they delivered to the Commander-in-Chief for the cause of the war?

"It was the character of their leader. Traveling with George Washington, observing him under all circumstances and conditions in battle and at ease, they took measure of their Commander-in-Chief. And what did they see? What were some of those outstanding qualities that glued the members of the Troop to Washington, eliciting their all to the point of great sacrifice?

"Whatever these qualities were, the cynical critics of George Washington have long tried to discredit them, but without very much success. [251]

"One hundred and fifty years after the Revolution, President Calvin Coolidge sat in his office in the White House one day, discussing these frantic attempts to demean the reputation of George Washington. Suddenly, President Coolidge wheeled his chair around and pointed to the great Washington Monument in the distance, a monument taller than the ancient Pyramids of Egypt, taller than the great spires of cathedrals. Then the President said: 'But George Washington is still there, in history. He still stands.' He is a man of heroic proportions, in spite of his periodic detractors.

"What were the qualities of Washington that caused the distinguished Napoleon to reverently bow his head when he first learned the sad news of Washington's death? What was it that led the British fleet, at the moment stationed in the English Channel, to fire a twenty gun salute in honor of the leader of a revolution which had defeated their own country? What did Washington reveal in his life and character that inspired England's great Gladstone to say:

" 'If among all the pedestals supplied by history for public characters of extraordinary nobility and purity I saw one higher than all the rest—and if I were requested to name the fittest occupant for it, I think my choice would have to light upon George Washington.'

"What were the qualities of the man which so impressed the members of the Troop and mankind in general?

"First of all, consider his humility.

" 'And when I saw it—I fell upon my face.'

"It could almost be said that George Washington had humility thrust upon him by natural circumstances.

"His Virginia family, though eminently respectable, did not rank with the grandees of the Virginia Colonies. He was not born with a sterling silver spoon in his mouth, but with only a silver-plated one that was quickly snatched away because of the death of his father when the boy was only eleven years old. Because of this, young Washington had to shift pretty much for himself. His father's property mostly went to his two half-brothers, Lawrence and Augustine. His brothers had gone to school in England, but George's mother, Mary Ball Washington, required his services and presence at home. His schooling was rather intermittent. He would never be allowed to go to college, and this lack had a deep effect upon him especially when, in later years, he dealt with college-bred men like Jefferson, for example.

"But he was able to learn vicariously and his brothers tutored him as best they could. By the age of sixteen, he had become a competent surveyor; he had developed skills in business and in farming. By the time he was twenty-one, he was the county surveyor, and he had picked up bargains in land, eventually owning some

[252]

5,000 acres in various sections of the south. He had leased Mount Vernon from his sister-in-law and would ultimately own it, especially after marrying a rich and attractive young widow by the time he was twenty-seven years of age. But he had begun his life under very humble circumstances; humility was particularly thrust upon him.

"But his humility was also the result of his growing awareness of God's presence in his life. 'And when I saw it, I fell upon my face.' He was a God-fearing man. He worshipped God in His church. There is a pew in this very church with a marker on it attesting to this fact. There were references in his writings to the effect that he felt a Divine Power outside himself, guiding him towards his destined place and inspiring his public service. He said once, 'To attempt government without God's help is impossible.'

"Washington remained fundamentally humble throughout his adult life.

"At the time the Continental Congress assembled to choose a Commander-in-Chief of the Colonial forces, knowing that he was under consideration, Washington wrote a friend that if he were chosen (and I quote): 'From that day I would date my fall and the ruin of my reputation.'

"When the Continental Congress selected him, he returned to the chamber of the Congress as requested, and he spoke as follows:

" 'Mr. President, though I am truly sensible of the high honor done me, yet I feel great distress from a consciousness that my abilities and my miltary experience may not be equal to this extensive and important trust. However, as the Congress desires, I will enter upon the momentous duty and exert every power I possess for the support of this glorious cause.'

"The first members of this Troop supported him and gave of themselves financially, not only because they believed in the cause but because they adored the man and

[253]

his humility. He seemed to express the warning St. Paul had given his followers 'Not to think more highly of themselves than they ought to think.'

"It was Tennyson who once said: 'Humility is the only true attitude of the human soul.'

"And the distinguished Ruskin once observed: 'The first test of a truly great man is his humility.'

"And the second quality possessed by George Washington, which must have impressed the members of this Troop who served with him, was a noble self-respect. Once again, from the Book of Ezekiel: 'Son of man, stand upon they feet.' In other words, 'Do not be stripped of all conscious worth. Be strong in an awareness of your innate worth to God and to man.' Be never prostrate upon the ground in a Uriah Heap sham humility but always erect, ready to cooperate with God and one's own countrymen when needed. God can hold little conversation with a person who is puffed up with empty pride, but when one cultivates his own self-courtesy and self-respect, God can speak to his own and use such a person for his great purposes.

"Noble self-respect was a strong quality in Washington's life. It was felt by those who knew him that, initially, caution and daring were close to a balance in his character. However, as military venture after military venture succeeded, he became increasingly disposed to take chances. As his self-respect firmed the more, he seemed to say to his men, 'We overcame that big obstacle yesterday and we can surely triumph over this new one today.' His self-respect was contagious, and enough of his officers and men caught it to keep a sufficient number of active soldiers in service, despite the rigors of Valley Forge, and ultimately to win the war.

"He made his men aware of their sacred cause, the need to maintain strength of character and thus win their great adventure of freedom.

"What a lesson we could learn from the noble self-respect exhibited by Washington.

"In our present time many influences seem determined to tear down men's self-respect. Today, our secular world glibly and freely offers us the bread of cynicism. It spreads before our young people cheap, vulgar and often pornographic food for the mind and the soul—cleverly seeking to lower one's self-respect, one's personal standards and one's ideals. And this can ultimately be deadly to the individual, as well as to the nation. It was Nietzsche who once truly said: 'If a man looks long enough into the dark abyss, surely the abyss will begin to look into him.'

"When men and women—boys and girls—go wrong it is because they forget their great intrinsic worth to themselves, to their nation and to their Creator. Self-respect continually asks a citizen in these degrading and strenuous times: 'Is this pattern of thought and behaviour good enough for you?'

"Today, America needs a sincere revival of personal self-respect on the part of all of our citizens, old and young. We need to recapture a new pride in our great personal and national lineage. 'Son of man—stand upon thy feet.'

"The third fundamental attitude which the first members of the Troop must have seen in their Commander-in-Chief was a deep human sympathy.

"Again, we look at the Prophet Ezekiel for our lead. The great Prophet had heard the call of God ordering him to go down to the Valley of the Euphrates and minister to his countrymen long in captivity there; people who had been cut off from their homeland and were now in slavery, a people now considered by those back home to be backsliders.

"Ezekiel did not relish his assignment. But because he was under orders, he went. When he reached his destination, he said very little. He listened intently. He identified himself with these people in their cruel suffering and in their despondency. His sympathy flowed out to them in an unlimited amount. When he did speak to them, he spoke with deep understanding. He actually suffered with them in their accursed exile during his visit. And returning home, he gave this report concerning his experience with his exiled fellow-countrymen: 'I sat where they sat.'

"George Washington was endowed with deep human sympathy. In dealing with his suffering, sick, discouraged men at Valley Forge, he showed his complete understanding of their difficulties. He held out at all times for the rights of his officers and men and insisted that they be treated as gentlemen. He constantly bolstered their morale. He counseled and comforted all those within his reach who needed his assistance. His deep sympathy held his men together through the most difficult months of suffering and deprivation.

"Washington's sympathy had also been known in his dealing with the slaves whom he had inherited. He hated the institution of slavery. He predicted that the nation would someday suffer war and ravage because of it. In a letter to Robert Morris, he wrote: 'No man living wishes more sincerely than I to see the abolition of slavery.' While he was still active both in Virginia and later as Commander-in-Chief, he secretly freed some of his slaves. When he died, his will ordered the freedom of all slaves belonging to his estate. No other man of his status did likewise so far as we know—certainly not Jefferson who had long been a severe critic of Washington.

"Human sympathy was one of his great qualities.

"My fellow Americans, we live in an exciting and crucial period of history. It is a time when our astronauts and our scientists have made us more aware of the other planets in our vast universe. Now God may have other great words for other planets, if perchance there is ultimately discovered that some of them are populated with people. But for our world with all of its woes and suffering, from the days of George Washington to the present time, God's great word for this world is sympathy. There are boys and girls, men and women, minorities, groups, ignored people, unfortunates, sick people suffering, whose needs must be recognized and met if we are ever to live together in this nation as a happy, united people. The weak must be lifted up and comforted by those who are strong. The sick must be healed by those who are skilled in the art of healing. This is not a matter of easy sentiment. It is one of intense enlightened obligation. It is part of God's divine plan of operation.

"For when God would give His greatest help to suffering humanity on this earth, what did He do? He had to become man to do it. The Infinite came down to our human nature, to sit where we sit in this sinful, troubled world.

"On Christmas Day, the word became flesh and dwelt among us. There was no other way, even for Almighty God. In Christ's ministry, He made humanity's ills His own, taking them even to the cross for us—that through Him men might be lifted up to God and be restored and made whole.

"Shakespeare's Iago cynically bade men to put their finances and human resources in a place of safekeeping to keep them for self. But Jesus of Nazareth, as Lord of Life, bade his followers to be generous to mankind through genuine and sacrificial sympathy.

"Humility. Self-respect. Sympathy. These three fundamental qualities so well exhibited in the life of George Washington, inspired Henry Lee to write convincingly of General Washington, that he was 'First in war, first in peace, and first in the hearts of his countrymen.'

"On this, the 175th anniversary of his death, let

us rejoice that George Washington's spirit still lives. He still stands in history as a great, dominant force. He still speaks to our people in terms completely understood by men and women, boys and girls of all races and conditions and traditions. Let us emulate him and bravely carry on as we enter the next century of our nation's existence.

"God save the United States of America."

Chapter 31

Farewell For Now

We live in a world of great change. There are many frightening things which give us pause. But again and again I am reminded of the Psalmist of old who wrote, "Where there are no changes, the people fear not God."

I think that, in view of the very troubled life we experience in our world, especially now in our own country, we need from time to time to listen to the wonderful prophet, Zechariah. This great Old Testament figure has been a constant source of inspiration to me throughout my ministry.

I am thinking at the moment of the eighth chapter of Zechariah, in which the prophet is describing the city of his dreams, the Jerusalem that he feels will one day evolve. Those of you who have read Zechariah will remember that the prophet, in this eighth chapter, predicts that peace will once again reign within the walls of the Holy City—that the problems of a social nature which are overpowering at the moment, will be solved and that prosperity and peace will return to the homes of the people. He speaks to a disillusioned group of followers, but in spite of their unbelieving eyes and ears he proceeds courageously to paint his picture of the future. He sees a happy, contented people, and a people made especially proud by troops of boys and girls growing in wisdom and stature—parents no longer fearful about rearing their children in a dangerous age. He speaks of a restored confidence in the land.

Of course, the picture which the prophet paints in this eighth chapter is in strange contrast to his times. At the moment he spoke, life had been very hard and the people were cynical. The struggle for existence was becoming much more hectic and, in reality, parents had very little encouragement to rear children at all. Life was dangerous. It was insecure. There seemed to be little hope.

But the prophet goes on to say that in the future this will all change. Conditions will marvelously improve. Men would, indeed, be able to fulfill their dreams and their destiny. Under God, he says, miraculous things are going to happen to benefit the people.

The reader will remember, of course, if he is familiar with Zechariah, that the prophet's prediction of things to come fell on most incredulous ears. The people were extremely tired, worried and uneasy. They were all but bankrupt in hope, and they did not try to conceal their cynicism as they listened to the prophet and as they expressed their doubts to one another.

But the prophet was not dismayed by their cynicism and doubts. Instead, he had an answer for his people, and his answer, I think, is one which we might well heed today. He said, "If it is wonderful in the eyes of the remnants of this people, in these times, should it also be wonderful in mine eyes? saith the Lord of Hosts." He goes on to ask, "Is not God the God of wonders, after all? Is not this His record in history?"

The prophet firmly believes that the wonders of man are God's wonders. He believes that God's commonplaces are man's marvels; that man's marvels are God's commonplaces. This was the burden of the argument used by the prophet Zechariah as he talked with the disspirited people of his time.

Well, how do we feel about this prophecy? Do we really believe that God is marvelous, and do we have any justification for believing that our problems will be solved? Is God a God of miracles? Can we believe this nowadays?

First, we ought always to consider as evidence God's miracle of existence. In our day, some men are inclined to dispute the miracles of Jesus as recorded in the New Testament. Some skeptics say on occasion, "Miracles just do not happen."

On the contrary, they happen all the time—if you mean by "miracle" that which defies our human analysis and goes beyond our human comprehension. Every flower, every blade of grass, every motion of one's body in obedience to one's will, is a miracle. Existence itself—the fact that we are—is a miracle. We cannot follow any growing thing to its origin without finding ourselves in the presence of a divine mystery of miraculous proportions.

Every morning, God says, "Let there be light" and you have a repetition of the first day of creation. Each spring, God says, "Let the earth bring forth the grass and herb, yielding seed after its kind." And behold, here again is the miracle of the sprouting seed and the full bud. God says, "Let us make man in our own image, after our likeness" and God continues to create man from generation to generation. The birth of each little baby is as mysterious as the creation of the first Adam. Existence itself is a miracle.

Even the works of men astonish us by their novelty and their wonder. Telstar is a miracle. We who have lived in Delaware have seen a miracle wrought in the discovery of nylon and other miraculous fabrics. Science is constantly enabling us to see more clearly that the great, divine commonplaces of God are the miracles of man.

And then too, we think of God's guidance of our human life. How wonderfully God has led us through the years. Thinking back over my own life, I readily confess that the best things have come to me through no planning or merit of my own whatever. I can honestly say that a wisdom not of my own creation has directed my steps and blessed my life with wonderful things—things that have happened to me far beyond my own desserts. A strength not my own has supported me through the crises of life, and this is true of everyone's life today. No matter how marvelous these have seemed to us, they are God's routine. He leads the blind by a path that they do not understand themselves. He holds in His hands the threads by which men weave the web of their own lives and the web of history. And He holds these threads so as to control the pattern of the weaving, in a way far beyond our comprehension. God is indeed a God of miracles.

Think of the marvelous things that are happening today. The development of the ecumenical movement, given great impetus by the late Pope John XXIII, is an extraordinary miracle which is bound to change the world in time.

Consider the moral miracles in men's lives. Is there anything more wonderful than the conversion of a sinner? The righting of the life of an alcoholic? Is there anything more remarkable or inspiring than the voluntary seeking of God by men and women, especially young people today who have every reason not to seek God and His truths?

When we actually see young women today resisting the temptations thrown at them by our society because they believe in a God whom they have never seen—when we think how men and women of today, clay like ourselves, remain steadfast in their faith and in their moral behavior in these times of great temptations and uncertainty, then I say this is a miracle indeed. This is a marvelous sight, and the prophet Zechariah, I think, was quite justified in predicting that miracles happen under the providential guidance of God, Who is a God of wonders.

I know there are many lay people today who are quite discouraged. They are discouraged about the church, discouraged about our country. I will admit that some of the clerical leadership in the church has been rather fuzzy and uncertain, and that the leadership in the nation has been confused or debased. I know that there are laymen, even in Delaware, who are somewhat disturbed and discouraged today about the future of the church. They need not be!

As I write these words, the diocese is anticipating the consecration of its eighth Bishop. In late January of 1975 the diocesan convention, meeting in St. David's Church, on Grubb Road in Brandywine Hundred (a parish I started as an act of faith, and which grew miraculously into one of the chief parishes in the diocese) elected the Reverend William Hawley Clark the eighth Bishop of Delaware. A review of the Bishop-Elect's record will reveal that he is well equipped for his new position. Bishop Clark has had extensive experience as a parish rector, in the midwest and in New England, and is therefore well versed in the requirements of the parish and the pastoral ministry. But in addition to this, and quite providentially, he has served in ecumenical posts and, at the hour of his election, he was the ecumenical officer of Worcester County in Massachusetts, heading a program supported by representative Christian churches in that area. Indeed, he was carrying forward the movement of Christian unity which was originated in our church by the renowned Bishop Charles H. Brent, and which was given enormous impetus by the late Pope John XXIII.

The diocese under Bishop Clark will continue to grow as it has in the past. The State of Delaware also has a great future. New Castle County alone is one of the fastest-growing areas in the country; and the Episcopal Church, with its long history in this state, is going to do things in the future which will be considered miraculous by the standards of the past in concert, of course, with other Christian bodies.

Under the new Bishop, the Episcopal Church will so conduct her affairs in the future that this communion will continue to bring about a greater degree of Christian unity in the Protestant world, and also there will be increasing unity with the Roman Catholic and the Greek Orthodox communions one day. I can also foresee increasing understanding between Christians and Jews.

We can even go so far as to predict that in the next fifty years America will return to religion, that this country will become, in the eyes of the world, a spiritually-minded nation again. We can predict, I believe, that the threats to world peace will pass; that with a greater understanding among peoples, with a greater role to be played by the United Nations, through education and through economic inter-relationships, nations will come to a better understanding of the importance of inter-dependence and cooperation. I know this sounds rather extraordinary, but I believe it is possible, under the God of Wonders, the God of Miracles!

Yet I can quite well imagine that some people reading these words will say, "Now wait just a moment. Let's be reasonable. Not so fast." Well, let's reason from past experience, if you wish to.

What would have been the status of the world, or the church, if history had always been determined by previous experience? There would have been no Jesus Christ of Bethlehem. The Christian Church would never have come into existence. History would have been frozen at its source. What lunatic would have predicted that the man condemned to die on the ignominious cross by Pontius Pilate would soon be raised to an honor, and a greatness, enjoyed by no Caesar that Rome ever knew? That Jesus would become the ideal of the human race? Alas, it is a human frailty for all of us to measure God's tomorrow by man's feeble yesterday.

Because we are tired and worried and disillusioned at times, we are inclined to stop in our personal striving and aspiration just when God is ready to begin to lead us on to new achievements. So many of us reduce Christian living to a mechanical pegging away day after day. What we need is to be delivered today from this peril. We need to be rescued from the dull, leaden weight of cynicism.

We all need to live constantly in the expectation that God is about to do wonderful things for us personally, for our nation, for our church and for our world. We need to believe that our greatest difficulties are actually going to be overcome. We do not know just when, but they are going to be overcome; we need to believe that the greatest evils of our world and society can be put down, if our efforts are really sincere and intelligent and inspired by God's own leadership. We need to believe again in God's marvelous operation.

Of course, I realize there will be many disappointments along the way. But after all, the reason for the disappointments will be this: not that we trusted too much in the God of the ages, the God of miracles; not that what we longed for was too good to be true, but rather it was not good enough! For one can never take too bright a view of his own spiritual life, of his own future, of society's future, the community's future, or that of the church, or the world, if in the center of it all we place Almighty God, the God of wonders, the God of miracles, who has brought us and our society to this point, and who is ready to take us much further than we can ever conceive at a given point in time.

Or, in the prophecy of the prophet Zechariah, "If it be marvelous in our eyes, is it neccessarily marvelous in the eyes of Him who is a God of wonders, omnipotent and all powerful, who is able to do exceeding abundantly above all that man can possibly think or ask?"

This is our God I am talking about. He is alive. He is working out His purpose. And in these most trying and difficult days, we need desperately to experience again in our hearts an understanding of the power and sustaining love of Almighty God, the God of Miracles.

With these thoughts, I, the old fifth Bishop of the Diocese of Delaware, say to my dear family and my beloved friends, "Adios. Farewell."

God bless you, each one!

10/17D